Congressional Papers
Management

Congressional Papers Management

*Collecting, Appraising, Arranging
and Describing Documentation of
United States Senators, Representatives,
Related Individuals and Organizations*

by FAYE PHILLIPS

McFarland & Company, Inc., Publishers
Jefferson, North Carolina, and London

British Library Cataloguing-in-Publication data are available

Library of Congress Cataloguing-in-Publication Data

Phillips, Faye
    Congressional papers management : collecting, appraising,
arranging and describing documentation of United States senators,
representatives, related individuals and organizations / by Faye
Phillips.
        p.   cm.
    Includes bibliographical references and index.
    ISBN 0-7864-0242-3 (library binding : 50# alk. paper) ∞
    1. United States.   Congress — Archives — Administration —
Handbooks, manuals, etc.   2. Legislators — United States — Archives —
Administration — Handbooks, manuals, etc.   I. Title.
CD3043.P48   1996
025.17'14 — dc20   96-13036
                                                             CIP

Manufactured in the United States of America

*McFarland & Company, Inc., Publishers
   Box 611, Jefferson, North Carolina 28640*

Acknowledgments

I would like to thank Jennifer Cargill, Dean of Libraries, and Robert S. Martin, Associate Dean for Special Collections, Louisiana State University, for their support of this project. The university made it possible for me to complete the manuscript through a sabbatical, for which I am grateful. The staff of the Louisiana and Lower Mississippi Valley Collections have been supportive, patient, and kind, and I appreciate their continued help. I would especially like to thank Merna W. Ford, whose excellent work with the Senator Russell B. Long Collection made much of this book possible. I would also like to thank John Bruce for his help and support.

There are many colleagues who work with congressional papers who have suggested ideas, shared experiences, edited sections, and given encouragement. The members of the Society of American Archivists Congressional Papers Roundtable have been especially helpful. Most particularly I would like to acknowledge the assistance given by Karen Dawley Paul of the United States Senate Historical Office; Cynthia Pease Miller of United States House of Representatives Historian's Office; Herbert Hartsook of the University of South Carolina; David A. Hales and Gretchen Lake of the University of Alaska–Fairbanks; Sheryl B. Vogt of the Richard B. Russell Library for Political Research and Studies; Jim Cross of the Strom Thurmond Institute of Clemson University; Naomi L. Nelson of Emory University; Ben Rogers of Baylor University; Alan Virta of Boise State University; Karyl Winn of the University of Washington; Mark Greene of the Minnesota Historical Society; Ron Peters, Todd Kosmerick and Janice Matthews of the Carl Albert Congressional Research and Studies Center; and John Caldwell of Louisiana Tech University, formerly with the Carl Albert Center.

Contents

Preface

In 1985 I began working in the United States Senate as a contract archivist for Senators who had decided to retire. My job was to help the Senators decide on a repository to send their papers to, review the papers in the offices and in storage, manage the records, help the staff members prepare their office files for transfer, and perform all the other tasks inherent in managing large archives of twentieth century congressional papers.

Luckily, I could turn to the Senate Historical Office and Senate Archivist Karen Paul for assistance. Karen's *Records Management Handbook for Senators* was an invaluable aid in preparing the files for transfer to their appropriate repositories. When an office had been following the records schedules in the *Handbook*, the work involved in closing the office was greatly diminished. Unfortunately, only one of the four offices in which I was working had done this. Therefore, appraisal had to be completed for most of the files before they could be sent to the repositories. In the limited time before the Senators left office not everything could be completed, so hundreds of boxes of files were sent to the repositories for complete appraisal and final processing.

One of those collections was that of Senator Russell B. Long of Louisiana. Senator Long's office had applied the records schedules in the *Handbook* and had employed a professional archivist (Patty Aronsson) for several years. Still, the 38 years of Senator Long's Senate career left, after appraisal, over 800 record center boxes that were sent to Louisiana State University. In December of 1986 I also went to Louisiana State University as curator of the Louisiana and Lower Mississippi Valley Collections, which was to be the home of Senator Long's papers. On December 3, 1995, we held the official opening of the Russell B. Long Collection and presented the published guide. During the ten years in which staff members of the Louisiana and Lower

Mississippi Valley Collections worked on the papers, they arranged, described, weeded, unfolded and flattened, and prepared finding aids for all the series in the collection including a large body of family papers which came in addition to the senatorial papers. Although permanent staff members were assigned to processing Senator Long's papers, they had other duties as well. All staff time spent on the project — professional, paraprofessional and student — averaged about 25 hours per week for ten years. Because of the importance of the Long family to the history of Louisiana, much more time was spent on this collection than will ever be spent on another. In this book I discuss the methodology used at LSU to determine the time to be allocated to congressional papers in the future.

As work progressed on Senator Long's collection, the Congressional Archivists Roundtable of the Society of American Archivists completed a project to prepare a documentation strategy for the Congress. Karen Paul served as project director and editor of *The Documentation of Congress: Report of the Congressional Archivists Roundtable Task Force on Congressional Documentation.* For that project and publication I wrote the section on documenting representation which discusses the disposition of senatorial office files.

My work with the congressional documentation project and with Senator Long's papers, as well as several consultancies to other congressional repositories, led to the present publication. The notes I prepared regarding decisions made for appraisal of congressional papers while in Washington, the decisions we made as we worked through Senator Long's files, and the needs I saw at other institutions convinced me that a manual to assist congressional archivists in their work was truly needed. Staff at the Louisiana and Lower Mississippi Valley collections also needed a manual they could follow, especially since less and less of my time could be spent working directly with the congressional collections. I was fortunate to be encouraged by many of my colleagues.

In this book archivists will find information on collecting policies for congressional papers and methods for applying the appraisal guidelines in Paul's *Handbook.* Arrangement suggestions are made for each series in a congressional collection and examples are given for describing the series and for writing the collection inventory. Included as well are methodologies for sampling series, an overview of electronic records found in congressional offices and a bibliography. The volume is illustrated with useful forms from several congressional repositories and also includes guidelines and procedures used at those repositories and at the Louisiana and Lower Mississippi Valley collections.

I do not attempt to answer philosophical questions regarding the future research use of congressional papers, although I believe they are a critical part of American history. I do presume that repositories collecting congressional papers have made the necessary commitments to process, house and make the collections available for research. I hope this book will assist many of the archivists in those repositories.

Introduction

"Large number in Congress calling it quits," read a headline in *The Baltimore Sun*, January 30, 1994. Thirty-three — a record number so early in the year — House of Representatives members announced their intention not to seek re-election.[1] This trend has continued and by April 1996, 32 House of Representatives members had announced retirement and 13 Senators planned retirement. In addition, 16 other members of the House planned to run for other offices or were defeated in primaries. Each representative who leaves Congress and every new representative or senator who comes to Congress creates office files. Such files and the activities of Congress they document are a part of American history.

What becomes of their office files when a representative or senator leaves Congress through election defeat, retirement, or death? The office closes and files are boxed, but where do they go? What steps are necessary to transfer papers for preservation? Which files are archivally valuable and which are not? Can records management practices be applied? Are there guidelines to follow that could answer such questions? Finally, who is responsible for answering these questions and implementing the necessary actions?

By tradition the office files — the papers — of members of Congress are considered to be personal papers. Since files from congressional offices are personal papers, who is responsible for their care? The office staff and the senator or representative must assume responsibility for establishing a records management plan for the office and for the preservation of historically valuable materials. They are also responsible for locating a proper repository for the housing and care of the papers. The repository is responsible for final appraisal, arrangement, description, and making the collection available for research use.

The Center for Legislative Archives at the National Archives and Records

1

Administration is responsible for the preservation of the official records of Congress while members and their staffs are responsible for the management of the information created in their offices. The Library of Congress holds congressional papers of various individuals but most are preserved in archival repositories across the country. Hundreds of libraries, historical societies, and non-profit agencies collect, appraise, arrange, describe and make these collections available for research. The *Guide to Research Collections of Former United States Senators 1789–1995* lists 594 repositories that hold papers representing men and women who have served in the United States Senate from 1789 to 1995. *A Guide to Research Collections of Former Members of the United States House of Representatives 1789–1987* lists 592 repositories which contain historical material on approximately 330 former members. Over 10,000 men and women, however, served in the U.S. House of Representatives from 1789 to 1987 and papers have been located for only 3,300 of them. Papers not currently in archival repositories must be cared for when and if they are found.[2]

Discussions have taken place regarding the need for the preservation of congressional papers and the methods for accomplishing the tasks involved.

> The 1978 Conference on the Research Use and Disposition of Senators' Papers affirmed the value inherent in senatorial papers. In the years since the conference, archivists and senate staff have struggled with preservation and use questions relating to those papers. In a continuing effort to answer such questions, the Dirksen Congressional Center and the National Historical Publications and Records Commission (NHPRC) sponsored a conference on congressional papers at Harper's Ferry, West Virginia, in 1985. The final *Congressional Papers Project Report* summarizes the findings of the Harper's Ferry conference and makes recommendations to the NHPRC on funding congressional papers projects. Germane to the NHPRC recommendations are minimum standards for congressional collections and repositories which accept congressional collections.[3]

The *Congressional Papers Project Report* delineates minimum standards for repositories collecting congressional papers, recommends better records management practices in congressional offices, suggests ways to attain better relationships between congressional offices and repositories, and supports specialized training for congressional archivists.[4] Previously, the attendees at the Conference on the Research Use and Disposition of Senators' Papers had also discussed points to be used in preserving senate papers. The 1978 conference emphasized the need for records management, early contact with a repository, minimum standards for repositories, limitation of restrictions, ease of access, reduction of bulk, and provided a "Checklist: Steps Toward

Establishing a Records Disposition Program."[5] The "Checklist" mirrors issues raised by the Harper's Ferry conference and a similar list now appears in the *Records Management Handbook for United States Senators and Their Repositories.*[6]

The minimum repository standard most stressed by historian William Leuchtenburg in the 1978 conference was the repository's ability to process papers. Leuchtenburg argued that congressional papers should not be given to small, understaffed libraries because travel to them is difficult and their ability to process papers is minimal. All historians at the conference were concerned that collections be acquired by repositories with professionally trained archivists because proper arrangement and description affect research use more profoundly than other factors.[7]

The 1978 Conference on the Research Use and Disposition of Senators' Papers passed a resolution which challenged archivists, historians, and congressional staff:

> Recognizing that the Conference has illuminated important problems of acquisition, research use, organization, processing, arrangement, description, and size of papers of United States senators, be it further resolved that this Conference urge that these and related questions receive further systematic study by representatives of the Senate, of the historical profession, and of the archival profession, through a study group sponsored by the Senate Historical Office and the Society of American Archivists.[8]

In September 1994, archivists, historians, congress men and women and congressional staff members convened again to "revisit the issues, to reassess the problems, to survey the progress made, and to speculate on the future of managing congressional archives."[9] Papers presented at the "Preservation, Use, and Accessibility of the Personal Papers of Members of Congress" conference reiterated that much work still remains as do many problems. However, attendees noted progress in the documentation of Congress, the work of the Center for Legislative Archives and the work of the SAA Congressional Papers Roundtable, as well as important publications.

Archivists, historians, and congressional staff are still struggling with concerns raised by the conferences. Through a number of books, reports and articles, professionals working with congressional papers have sought to establish answers to many of these questions (see bibliography). In 1984 archivist Patricia Aronsson published "Appraisal of Twentieth-Century Congressional Collections," in 1985 the first edition of Karen Dawley Paul's *Records Management Handbook for United States Senators and Their Repositories* appeared, the *Congressional Papers Project Report* was issued in 1986, and from 1988 to 1995 several other worthwhile articles appeared, as did the second edition of Paul's *Records Management Handbook*.[10] Publication of the proceedings of the 1994 Portland Conference is also planned.

A recent study concerned with congressional papers and their preservation is *The Documentation of Congress: Report of the Congressional Archivists Roundtable Task Force on Congressional Documentation*. The catalyst for this report was the 1989 conference "Understanding Congress: A Bicentennial Research Conference," sponsored by the U.S. Senate Commission on the Bicentennial, the Commission on the Bicentenary of the U.S. House of Representatives, and the Congressional Research Service of the Library of Congress. *The Documentation of Congress*:

> records the professional views and analyses of the individual contributors and task force members who are representative of the diverse groups sharing responsibility for preserving the documentary record of Congress. It is reproduced to assist them and others involved in the ongoing process of selecting, preserving and making available for research use congressional information of lasting value. Its purpose is to serve to stimulate discussions and to inspire future coordinated action in the preservation and research use of these valuable documentary resources.[11]

The Documentation of Congress also found that a great variation exists among the descriptive terminology in finding aids created for congressional papers by archivists, and that the archivists processing the collections vary in their level of comprehension of the legislative process. This comprehension is critical to the proper cataloging of congressional papers collections. The authors of the report are also concerned about the lack of processing for many important collections due to the minimal resources available to repositories for this work. More members of Congress need to add professional archival expertise to their staffs to aid the repositories in handling congressional papers. "Given the quantity of material that accumulates in an office, continuous identification and selection of potential archival materials is the only cost-effective way to ensure that information of long-term value will be preserved."[12]

All the above studies emphasize that further study and research are necessary regarding the preservation of congressional papers collections. Most agree that guidelines on appraisal, arrangement, description, and reference services are needed to assist the offices and the repositories. A manual on these topics will serve as a critical companion to the *Records Management Handbook for United States Senators and Their Repositories*, the House of Representatives' "Guidelines for the Disposition of Members Papers," and *The Documentation of Congress*.[13] This manual seeks to fill that void.

The historical record inherent in these collections is critical to the study of politics, economics, society, and Congress. Every senator and representative must accept the responsibility to preserve their records, and repositories must work with these offices in order to benefit scholars and students. Because the preservation of these papers is so very important for the full documentation of American life, archivists and congressional offices need guidelines to follow in the appraisal, arrangement, description, and research use of these collections. This book has been written to assist in the preservation of congressional documentation.

NOTES

1. Karen Hosler, "Large number in Congress calling it quits," *Baton Rouge Sunday Advocate*, January 30, 1994, 1A, 9A.

2. Karen Dawley Paul, Compiler, *Guide to Research Collections of Former United States Senators, 1789–1995*, S. Pub. 103-35 (Washington, D.C.: United States Senate, 1995); Cynthia Pease Miller, editor-in-chief, *A Guide to Research Collections of Former Members of the United States House of Representatives 1789–1987*, House Doc. 100–171 (Washington, D.C.: United States House of Representatives, 1988), ix.

3. Faye Phillips, "Harper's Ferry Revisited: The Role of Congressional Staff Archivists in Implementing the Congressional Papers Project Report," *Provenance*, 6, (Spring 1988): 26–47.

4. Frank Mackaman, *Congressional Papers Project Report* (Washington, D.C.: National Historical Publications and Records Commission, 1986), 17–27.

5. J. Stanley Kimmitt and Richard A. Baker, *Conference on the Research Use and Disposition of Senators' Papers Proceedings* (Washington, D.C.: United States Senate, 1978), 3.

6. Phillips, "Harper's Ferry Revisited," 28–29.

7. Kimmitt and Baker, *Proceedings*, 21, 69.

8. *Ibid.*, 121.

9. L. Rebecca Johnson Melvin, "Congressional Papers Conference, Portland, Maine, 1994," Society of American Archivists Congressional Papers Roundtable *Newsletter*, November 1994, 2.

10. Also important is the "Advisory Committee on the Records of Congress, First Report, December 31, 1991" (Washington, D.C.: National Archives and Records Administration, Center for Legislative Archives, 1991), and the "Second Report, December 1995."

11. Karen Dawley Paul, Project Director, *The Documentation of Congress: Report of the Congressional Archivists Roundtable Task Force on Congressional Documentation*, S. Pub. 102-20 (Washington, D.C.: United States Senate, 1992), i.

12. *Ibid.*, 14, 3.

13. Karen Dawley Paul, *Records Management Handbook for United States Senators and Their Repositories* (Washington, D.C.: United States Senate, 1992); Cynthia Pease Miller, "Guidelines for the Disposition of Members' Papers," United States House of Representatives Historical Office, 1991; and Paul, *The Documentation of Congress*.

CHAPTER 1

Collecting Congressional Papers

Many institutions throughout the country have assumed the responsibility for acquiring, preserving and making available for research the papers of United States senators and representatives. Some of these repositories care for the papers of all senators and representatives from their state, current as well as historical. Most states have a diversity of institutions that care for congressional papers. In Louisiana there are five institutions that maintain congressional papers collections. In New York there are approximately 31 separate repositories that accept congressional papers. For those institutions that still acquire congressional papers, the challenges are great. If the papers are from a senator or representative long out of office they will evidence the same problems that all uncared for manuscripts and archives have: disorder, damage from insects and environmental conditions, and incompleteness. If the repository acquires papers from sitting senators and representatives, other problems occur as well. The repository acquiring such collections must accept responsibility for the proper transfer of materials, the arrangement and description of the collections, and the requirement to make the materials available to researchers within a reasonable time.

Processing congressional papers and making them available for research is costly. Repositories must consider the financial consequences of acquiring them. In most cases the repositories have assumed the costs associated with processing, preservation and housing, and reference for these materials. Many times the congressperson or their family will provide funding assistance for the care of the papers or provide an endowment for the continued maintenance of the papers. Congress has in the past provided limited funding for the preservation of the papers of former House Speakers. The families of former Senator Richard B. Russell of Georgia and former Representative Claude Pepper of Florida have provided funds for endowments that support the repositories that house their papers. In Alaska, the state legislature has provided some funding for the care of congressional papers. Many other senators and representatives have provided funding for published guides, preservation needs, and research stipends for their repositories. A repository that plans on collecting congressional papers should not expect funding from any of these sources, however. In most cases the repository will bear the financial responsibility for all activities related to congressional papers. Despite the lack of outside funding sources, the preservation of congressional papers is an important and valuable need.

Collection Development Policies

Today in conjunction with the excellent documentation strategy for Congress published in 1992, congressional papers archivists need to refine repository collection development policies to focus on subject areas. Connell Gallagher, writing about the "Problems of the Collection Development Archivist," says it best: "The lack of a collection policy can be detrimental, for it is almost impossible to make progress in processing, grant writing, or reference service if the collection has no focus."[1] Although Gallagher's comment refers to all collecting activities of a repository, it is more than applicable to congressional papers collections.

The Documentation of Congress immensely aids the work of congressional papers archivists and the repositories that collect such papers.[2] The report presents a viable, working documentation strategy for the Congress. Included are definitions, sources and status of documentation, and recommended actions for congressional functions. As part of the overall documentation strategy, the task force recommends the writing of a model policy statement "for archival institutions that are interested in specializing in congressional/legislative/political research."[3]

One of the minimum standards stated for a congressional papers repository by the *Congressional Papers Project Report* authors is that it have an appropriate collecting policy. These minimum standards can, of course, be prioritized in many different ways, but thorough planning necessitates that appropriate collecting policies be the first priority.

Too often, congressional papers go to repositories because of political commitments, not because of the ability of the repository to care for the papers. Political commitments are not always preventable by congressional staffs or archivists. However, a written collecting policy approved by the repository's administration will do much to avert unwanted commitments. Written collection development policies and planning have as their main goal the diminishing of unwanted events.

> Written and institutionally accepted collecting policies help to prevent such problems as do acknowledged documentation strategies. Few university administrators will ever attempt to learn about the collecting policies of the manuscripts department, but if those policies are written and endorsed officially, then the manuscript department can more ably combat political commitments which hamper the abilities of the department. This requires archivists to provide collecting policies and to push them through administrative approval.[4]

Effective policies are reflective of the objectives and plans of the organization; consistent; flexible, so they can be changed as new needs arise; distinguished from rules and procedures (policies allow for latitude but rules and procedures remain firm); and written. The model established for written collecting policies contains the following elements:

I.   Statement of purpose of the institution and/or collection.

II.   Types of programs supported by the collection
       A. Research
       B. Exhibits
       C. Community outreach
       D. Publications
       E. Others (specify)

III.   Clientele served by the collection
       A. Scholars and professionals
       B. Graduate students
       C. Undergraduates
       D. General public
       E. Other (specify)

IV.   Priorities and limitations of the collection
       A. Present identified strengths
       B. Present collecting level
       C. Present identified weaknesses
       D. Desired level of collection to meet program needs
       E. Geographical areas collected
       F. Chronological periods collected
       G. Subject areas collected

The detailed congressional papers collection development policy should be written into the overall policy under Section IV. Priorities and limitations of the collection, G. Subject areas collected. A manuscripts repository may be geographically oriented with many strong subject areas.[6] (See APPENDIX: Collection Development Policy, Richard B. Russell Library for Political Research and Studies, University of Georgia Libraries.) However, to refine the collection development policy, these subject areas need further delineation.[7]

MODEL CONGRESSIONAL PAPERS COLLECTION DEVELOPMENT POLICY

In order to more fully meet its mission the _____ will collect the personal papers of this state's congressional delegation except those discussed in collecting policy section IV. Priorities and limitations of the collection, J. Exclusions.

CONGRESSIONAL PAPERS DEFINITION:

Congressional papers are by tradition considered to be personal papers which may be acquired by universities, historical societies and libraries. These papers are created in the offices of United States Senators and House of Representatives Members by the senator or representative and their staffs. This includes papers from all Congresses since 1789.

PARAMETERS:

This repository will collect the papers of any elected or appointed senator or representative from the state of _____ including those which served in any Congress since 1789 up to the present. The only papers which will not be accepted are covered in the section on exclusions.

CRITERIA FOR ACCEPTANCE:

All congressional papers (for current members, past members post–1950s and past members pre–1950s) must meet the following criteria to be accepted by this repository[8]:

1. A deed of gift or deposit agreement is signed.

2. Only limited and reasonable restrictions are requested.

3. The files are complete for the congressional period and pre-congressional papers are included.

4. The Member of Congress served a significant number of years and/or was involved in events of historical importance that give the papers extensive research value.

5. When electronic records system documentation exists along with texts and indexes, those electronic records can be accessed through the repository's computers. Paper back-up systems exist where appropriate for electronic records.

6. Appropriate files have been microfilmed and the microfilm is indexed and in good physical working condition.

7. Non-paper media items are identified, dated, indexed and in good physical condition.

8. The Member of Congress and his/her staff and family are willing to assist in oral history projects and in collecting the papers of ancillary persons and organizations.

9. The components of the papers are well defined and in good order, as well as in good physical condition.

10. The weedable series (series which might be sampled) are easily distinguished.

11. For sitting members of Congress, their office must have a current working records management plan.

ANCILLARY PERSONS AND/OR ORGANIZATIONS TO BE COLLECTED IN CONJUNCTION WITH CONGRESSIONAL PAPERS:

DEFINITION:

Congress is not an isolated organization. Thousands of individuals who are not members of Congress affect who is elected, what bills are presented and passed by Congress, the public's view of Congress, judicial efforts, fundraising and almost every aspect of what Congress is and does.

EXAMPLES:

The following are examples of the types of individuals and organizations that are ancillary to Congress:

- unsuccessful candidates in significant elections
- state and local political parties including temporary political associations
- noncongressional political organizations:
  - League of Women voters
  - ad hoc party groups
  - political consultants
  - special interest groups
  - political action committees (PACs)
  - state and local politicians
- judicial personnel
- media individuals and organizations
- lobbyists and lobbying groups
- public policy research organizations
- congressional scholars
- campaign volunteers

PARAMETERS:

This repository will collect the papers of ancillary individuals or organizations that significantly impacted the election, activities, voting, campaigns, media perceptions, etc. of elected or appointed Members of Congress from the state of _____ from 1789 up to the present.

CRITERIA FOR ACCEPTANCE:

Papers and records of ancillary individuals or organizations must meet the criteria established for the papers of members of Congress. Organizations currently in operation must have a working records management plan.

Congressional papers can be viewed in three chronological periods: sitting members, past members whose papers bulk in post–1950, and past members whose papers bulk in pre–1950. The nature of work and the way it is done in Congress have changed most dramatically since the 1950s, which leads to this appropriate division. Before World War II, Congress was essentially a part-time institution. Since World War II, Congress has become a full-time institution and congressional staff have increased from about 2,000 to 12,000. Karen Dawley Paul in *The Documentation of Congress* gives a thorough explanation of how the post–1950 Congress differs from the pre–1950 Congress. The major changes are the drastic increase of the work-load of Congress, the subsequent increase in size of the legislative branch, the evolution of committees and subcommittees and the trend toward greater decisionmaking and influence on the part of subcommittees, an increase in Congressional oversight activity, a greater reliance on staff, an increase in the number of informal groups within Congress which diffuses power, a proliferation of special interest groups outside Congress, and an opening of Congress to more thorough public scrutiny.[9]

Most repositories would collect any material found about the earliest senators or representatives from their states if such papers could be located. However, it is important to define this in the collection policy. The policy might include a statement that all materials created by 18th and 19th cen-tury Members of Congress from the state will be collected regardless of com-pleteness, etc.

Another important consideration in the division between pre– and post–1950 congressional papers is the creation and use of automated corre-spondence systems and computers, the development of local area networks, use of E-mail systems, and creation of biographical databases. In the post-1980s, E-mail and relational databases began to be used in most Senate offices. For example, Senator Russell B. Long of Louisiana was elected in 1948 and retired in 1986. Not until the late 1960s did the office employ any type of automated correspondence system. The Senate Computer Center's Correspondence Management System was not used in Long's office until 1982. Four years later, when he retired, all staff members in Long's office had a personal computer on their desk. Electronic records and their man-agement affect what records are created and how archivists deal with them.[10]

Collection development policies, documentation strategies and appraisal are interdependent. Strategies and policies identify the materials to be col-lected and contain the conditions the materials must meet in order to be acquired. Many of these conditions are appraisal decisions and appear in appraisal checklists as well as in criteria for acceptance and minimum stan-dards for collections.

The Records Management Handbook for United States Senators and Their Archival Repositories (1991), the House of Representatives' "Guidelines for Disposition of Members' Papers" (1992), and *The Documentation of Congress* are necessary aids in appraising congressional papers. Other helpful publica-tions are: *Guidelines for Standing and Select Committees in the Preparation, Filing, Archiving and Disposal of Committee Records* (1990), a Committee on House Administration Committee Print; *A Guide for the Creation, Organi-*

zation and Maintenance of Records in Congressional Offices (revised 1990) by the Library of Congress, Central Services Division; and the *Congressional Handbook*.[11]

The Records Management Handbook also assists in the difficult appraisal decisions associated with electronic records. The first edition of the handbook (1985) is helpful in understanding some of the older computer systems used in the Senate. Electronic records (machine readable records) have not eliminated paper files as once predicted. On the contrary, they have made the archivist's job more difficult, for all congressional offices have electronic records in addition to paper files.

Other criteria in the collection development policy may or may not be appraisal questions. However, appraisal cannot be completed unless these questions are answered.

Is there a signed deed of gift or deposit agreement? (See the following section on deeds of gift.) Are any required restrictions limited and reasonable? Many archivists will agree with the maxim that "no gift is ever free," and restrictions are one cost associated with manuscript collections. Members of Congress and their families may request that certain portions of personal materials be closed for a reasonable period of time to withhold sensitive information in order to protect living persons and to prevent libel. Archivists are faced with the requirements of the Federal Privacy Act and Freedom of Information Act, and in some cases with national security classified files that are restricted by statute. Although the personal papers of Members of Congress are not governed by these acts, most wish to adhere to the spirit of the laws. Finally, any photocopies of records of congressional committees are governed by House and Senate rules.[12] Original archival committee records are housed in the National Archives.

Is the member of Congress and his/her staff and family willing to assist in oral history projects and in collecting the papers of ancillary persons and organizations? The verbal nature of Congress is well covered in the *Documentation of Congress*, which recommends the establishment of oral history projects for all repositories collecting congressional papers in order to enhance the research value of such collections. The Carl Albert Congressional Research and Studies Center has published *Oral History Project: Procedure Manual* by Daniel J. Linke, which is an excellent model for other congressional repositories' oral history programs.[13]

The member of Congress or his/her family can also influence the collection of the papers of ancillary persons or organizations. See the next section for a discussion of the types of ancillary papers the collecting policy should include.

The appraisal of congressional papers is discussed in Chapter 2 and it cannot be overemphasized how closely appraisal and acquisition of appropriate materials are bound together. Appraisal is the subject of a substantial body of archival literature but collection development policies are not. The inclusion of ancillary papers of persons or organizations in the collection development policy for congressional papers was first discussed in *The Documentation of Congress*. Therefore, this section of the manual discusses in detail the collecting of materials ancillary to congressional papers. *The Documentation of Congress* recommends that the papers of ancillary persons and the records of ancillary organizations be part of the overall documentation strategy and that collecting policies for congressional papers include them.

Any ancillary persons and organizations can also be grouped under other subject areas collected by the repository; i.e. journalism, statewide organizations, minority groups, judiciary, state politics, etc. But they should be viewed with the congressional papers collection development policy in order to emphasize their relationships to congressional papers. The various groups included in this section represent the interrelationships and overlapping staffing that Congress and the political parties have with others.

The types of individuals and organizations that are ancillary to Congress may include some of the following:

Unsuccessful candidates in significant elections who document a point of view differing from the winner may offer material ancillary to congressional papers. At the national level, Ross Perot and George Wallace are good examples. At the state level, the papers of a defeated candidate for Congress who continues to play a role in state activities and might run for future office should be collected.

The records of state and local political parties/organizations includes temporary political associations, which can include state and local Democratic, Republican and third party (Socialist, Libertarian, etc.) organizations. Many congressional membership organizations also have a regional or local focus such as the Northeast-Midwest Legislative Service Organization. In some states a temporary political association such as the Louisiana "No Dukes" organization that opposed senatorial and gubernatorial candidate David Duke in the 1980s and 1990s may be ancillary. Just as important are "unofficial" congressional membership organizations (those that do not receive appropriated funds) which have regional or local interests.[14]

Noncongressional political organizations are excellent candidates for regional or statewide cooperative collecting policies.[15] These may include organizations which have as their goal the education of all voters regardless of party or non-party affiliation. The records of the League of Women Voters, a non-partisan, political education group, should be collected in all 50 states. Other non-partisan groups might be similar to the Public Affairs Research Council of Louisiana, whose only purpose is to educate voters. Special interest groups (e.g., Right to Life, Pro Choice, World Wildlife Fund, Louisiana Coalition Against Racism and Nazism) can affect congressional activities as well as influence voters whether national, regional, or local. They may affect voting by issue mail campaigns, running their own candidates for office, supporting think-tanks and political action committees (PACs), and lobbying. Their officers may be volunteers who hold the organizations' records and, if not collected quickly, the records may disappear when these groups are only temporary. Their records are difficult to locate but their activities are critical to compiling a complete picture.

While it often seems to the public that PACs are an official part of Congress, they are not. These committees are usually large financial campaign contributors and are required to report to the Federal Election Commission. They raise and make donations to campaigns and even finance advertising for and against candidates. They are sometimes attached to business or special interest groups. The financial influence they have had since the early 1970s has changed the way campaigns are run and has lessened the candidate's personal influence over campaigns. They can be categorized as corporate, labor, trade, membership, health, "nonconnected" (neither candidate nor party related), cooperative, and corporate without stock.[16]

Not surprisingly, state and local politicians also have influence with Congress, and their papers should be collected.[17] Many states legally require that the records of state and local officials be transferred to the state archives. When that is not the case, local repositories may collect them.

The papers of many consultants also add to the documentation of Congress. Political consultants work for a specific candidate or political party and their job is to get their candidate elected. Media consultants and political consultants change roles frequently. Individuals may also serve as lobbyists or think-tank employees when not working with a candidate.

The papers of those judges associated with particular politicians, parties or philosophies should be collected.[18] Also collect the papers of judges who assisted or opposed Congress in the development of legislation relating to the courts. Federal and Supreme Court justices' papers should be acquired at the state or national level as well.

Many media individuals and organizations focus on the functions of Congress and produce ancillary papers and records that repositories should acquire.[19] Individual legislative and political journalists in print, television and radio can be included, as can political cartoonists. Many repositories already have substantial collections of journalists' papers. Because these collections include all types of journalists, it is helpful to list legislative and political journalists in the collection development policy for congressional papers. Organizations such as the National Press Club advise journalists on appropriate repositories for their papers.

Most states have a state journalism association and large cities may have local ones. These membership organizations' records give an overview of policy concerns of state and local journalists and may include information on lobbying by these organizations.

Film, video and audio tapes from broadcasting stations that are political coverage or political programs are also valuable to a study of Congress. A repository cannot afford to collect the entirety of records from local TV and radio stations but could develop an agreement whereby one or two stations send appropriate political coverage to the repository. C-SPAN (Cable Satellite Public Affairs Network) broadcasting is collected at Purdue University Public Affairs Video Archives and copies of tapes can be purchased. The Vanderbilt University Television News Archives records, abstracts, and indexes national evening news broadcasts of ABC, NBC, CBS, and CNN Prime News. Copies are available.

The role of media consultants has become increasingly important in political campaigns and their papers will add to the historical record. Some congressional press secretaries become media consultants after leaving Congress. Media consultants still tend to stay behind the scenes in political activities (unlike James Carville), which makes their papers harder to collect. Public relations firms and advertising agencies also serve as media consultants.

In addition, the influence of lobbyists and lobbying groups has grown since World War II.[20] Numerous businesses, state officials, organizations and individuals lobby Congress at one time or another on issues important to them, but this section refers to professional lobbyists and full-time lobbying organizations. PACs may fall into this section as well. Many organizations' records contain lobbying information, e.g. the National Rifle Association, the National Association for the Advancement of Colored People, the American Library Association, and the American Association of Retired Persons.

Individual lobbyists who have long careers or organizations that have lobbied for a number of years will have the most complete files. Repositories should collect the papers of lobbyists and records of lobbying groups that are closely associated with issues that concern their state's congressional delegation. For example, Louisiana is economically dependent on the petroleum and chemical industries, therefore Louisiana repositories will want to collect files from the significant petroleum and chemical industries' lobbyists.

Often overlooked are the records of public policy research organizations (think tanks).[21] These are nongovernmental, nonprofit public policy organizations. Some have been around since the early 1900s but most have been established only since the 1960s. They may not legally lobby if they are registered as tax-exempt. Think tanks can be partisan or nonpartisan and individuals who have served as lobbyists, organization officers, politicians, consultants, and even congressional scholars move in and out of employment with these groups. Many legislative service organizations in Congress have affiliated private organizations which function as public policy organizations. For example, the Democratic Study Group supports the Democratic Study Center.[22]

University archives or manuscripts departments usually collect the papers of their professors who are congressional scholars, but those who are not affiliated with universities present papers which should be collected as well. Historians, political scientists, legal scholars, social scientists and faculty in mass communications may all study the history, activities and functions of the United States Congress. Most repositories collect faculty and scholars' papers, but those collecting congressional papers should also seek papers of independent scholars in their state who concentrate on the study of Congress.

Political campaigns have always been run with the help of volunteers. Volunteers work in campaigns, on committees, serve as part of special interest organizations, and in many other nonpaid capacities related to members of Congress. These volunteers may or may not become designated officials in the organizations they work for. In collecting ancillary papers to congressional collections, repositories should look for the evidence of volunteer activity in the papers of businessmen, educators, artists, journalists, and members of civic and community organizations (even garden club members).

All repositories operate more effectively with written collection development policies. If such policies are the foundation upon which the collection is built then documentation strategies provide the structural framework. *The Documentation of Congress* serves as the framework for repositories' congressional collections. This model collection development policy for congressional collections is a preliminary road map.

Deeds of Gift

Before accepting any congressional papers collection the repository must acquire from the congressperson or the family a deed of gift or a deposit agreement. Such a contract ensures that all parties understand their responsibilities regarding the collection.

A deed of gift or a deposit agreement can delineate the mutual expectations among the repository, the family, and the congressional office. It should include:

• a description of the donor and the receiver;
• an explanation of materials being given or deposited, including a brief list;
• inclusive dates and size of the materials;
• any restrictions on use and the time limit of the restrictions;
• who owns literary rights and copyrights;
• the allowable disposition of duplicate materials;
• expected time in which the repository will fully process the collection;
• allowable use of materials for research prior to completed processing;
• a description of additions; and
• whether finding aids or guides are to be produced.

The deed may state that duplicate materials may be discarded by the repository, that only classified materials will be restricted, and that literary and copyrights belong to the repository upon the death of the senator or representative. Future questions of ownership and obligations are clearly answered in a proper deed.[23]

Most repositories are now fully aware of the critical need for legally accurate and current contracts with donors detailing the terms of the gift or of the deposit. The deed protects the rights of the repository, the donors, and potential researchers. In the July 1993 issue of the Society of American Archivists newsletter, *Archival Outlook*, a draft American Library Association-Society of American Archivists "Joint Statement on Access to Original Materials in Libraries, Archives, and Manuscript Repositories" appeared. This statement should be used as a standard for deeds of gift. Examples of deeds of gift and deposit agreements can be found in Paul, *Records Management Handbook*.[24] Cynthia Pease Miller, Office of the Historian for the House of Representatives, has written a brochure on deeds of gift for members of Congress. Deposit agreements are sometimes the only agreement the repository is able to gain from the donor but caution is always required. As shown in Ronald L. Becker's case study, "On Deposit: A Handshake and A

Lawsuit," *American Archivist* 56 (Spring 1993): 320–328, the best of intentions can lead to ownership problems when no deed of gift is signed. By acquiring signed deeds of gift or deposit agreements such problems can be avoided.

NOTES

1. Connell Gallagher, "Problems of the collection development archivist," *AB Bookman's Weekly* 85:12 (March 19, 1990): 1225.

2. Paul, *The Documentation of Congress.*

3. *Ibid.*, 15.

4. Phillips, "Harper's Ferry Revisited," 37.

5. For a more thorough discussion of elements see: Faye Phillips, "Developing Collecting Policies" *American Archivist* 47 (Winter 1984): 30–42; for model collection development policies see Faye Phillips, *Local History Collections in Libraries* (Englewood, CO: Libraries Unlimited, 1995).

6. In addition to the policy from the Richard B. Russell Library for Political Research and Studies in the Appendix also helpful are: "Manuscript Collection Policies, Revised June 30, 1992," Special Collections Department, Bailey/Howe Library, University of Vermont; and Janice Mathews and Todd Kosmerick, "SAA Congressional Papers Roundtable Presentation on Collection Policy and Deed of Gift, September 1993," which relates to their work at the Carl Albert Congressional Research and Studies Center Archives at the University of Oklahoma.

7. Parts of the following section were first published by the author as "Congressional Collection Development Policies," in the *American Archivist*, (Summer 1995): and is published with permission of the Society of American Archivists.

8. Much of this section is drawn from Mackaman, *Congressional Papers Project Report*, 17–27.

9. Paul, *Documentation of Congress*, 17–21. Such change is so significant that the 1994 National Heritage Lecture in Washington was "Changing Congress" and addressed the changes in Congress and its membership since World War II. See: "Society to Host National Heritage Lecture," *The Capitol Dome*, 29 (Winter 1994): 1.

10. See Faye Phillips and Merna W. Ford, *Russell Billiu Long Collection Guide* (Baton Rouge, LA: Special Collections, Louisiana State University Libraries, 1995).

11. For a repository point of view see: Division of Library & Archives, Minnesota Historical Society, "Report of the Congressional Papers Appraisal Committee," 1993. Also very important to this discussion is Patricia Aronsson, "Appraisal of Twentieth-Century Congressional Collections," *Archival Choices*, edited by Nancy Peace (Lexington, MA: Lexington Books, 1984), 81–104.

12. It is recommended that House committee records have restricted access for 30 years and Senate committee records for 20 years. See Rules XI and XXXVI of the Rules of the House of Representatives, and Senate Rules XI and XXVI 10 (a), and S. Res. 474, 96th Congress.

13. Daniel J. Linke, *Oral History Project: Procedure Manual* (Norman, OK: Carl Albert Congressional Research and Studies Center, 1990).

14. See Gary Hoag, "Congressional Member Organizations," in Paul, *The Documentation of Congress*, 69–78.

15. See Aronsson, "Appraisal," 98–100.

16. Paul, *Documentation of Congress*, 48.

17. See Paul I. Chestnut, "Appraising the Papers of State Legislators," *American Archivist* 48 (1985): 167–178.

18. See James Cross, "Congress and the Judicial Branch," in Paul *The Documentation of Congress*, 91–98.

19. See Faye Phillips, "Congress and the Media," in Paul, *Documentation of Congress*, 99–104.

20. See Sheryl Vogt, "Congress and Lobbyists," in Paul, *The Documentation of Congress*, 105–112.

21. See Karen Paul, "Congress and Think Tanks," in Paul, *The Documentation of Congress*, 109–112.

22. Paul, *The Documentation of Congress*, 71, 159.

23. Phillips, "Harper's Ferry Revisited," 41.

24. Also see Trudy Peterson, "The Gift and the Deed," *American Archivist* 42 (January 1979): 61–66.

CHAPTER 2

Appraising Congressional Papers

The collection development policy criteria for acceptance of materials is the basis for appraisal guidelines. Appraisal determines which papers will come to the archives for permanent preservation.

Although congressional papers are traditionally viewed as personal papers, the office files can best be controlled by a records management plan while the member is in Congress. Archival appraisal and records management are closely tied.

Appraisal in archival terms is defined as "the process of determining the value and thus the disposition of records [papers] based upon their current administrative, legal, and fiscal use; their evidential and informational value; their arrangement and condition; their intrinsic value; and their relationship to other records [papers]."

Records management is defined as "a field of management responsible for the systematic control of the creation, maintenance, use, and disposition of records."[1]

The Documentation of Congress suggests that professional archivists need to be involved with congressional offices as early as possible. Some offices have assumed responsibility for processing their collections while in Washington but many more have made few plans for archival disposition. "Given the quantity of materials that accumulates in an office, continuous identification and selection of potential archival materials is the only cost-effective way to ensure that information of long-term value will be preserved."[2]

Other publications useful to the appraisal of congressional papers include Gerald Ham, *Selecting and Appraising Archives and Manuscripts*;

Nancy E. Peace, *Archival Choices: Managing the Historical Record in an Age of Abundance*; Frank Mackaman, *Congressional Papers Project Report*; Faye Phillips, "Harper's Ferry Revisited: The Role of Congressional Staff Archivists in Implementing the Congressional Papers Project Report"; Karen D. Paul, *The Documentation of Congress*; and the Minnesota Historical Society's, Division of Library and Archives, "Report of the Congressional Papers Appraisal Committee."

Congressional offices operate somewhat like individual businesses. Aronsson calls congressional papers collections hybrids, "neither strictly archival nor strictly personal." Since each congressional office focuses on the needs of a single state or congressional district, one unmodifiable, standard records schedule will not work for all members of Congress. Traditional formulas need revisions to make these collections useful.[3] Gallagher found that congressional papers "were really the records of an organization rather than an individual," even though they revolved around a unique individual. In some cases it seems that the papers document the activities of the staff who do the work rather than the member. The member's job is to present his view of legislation in committee, on the floor, to the public, persuade other members to accept the legislation he supports, and vote.[4]

Although each senator and representative has similar responsibilities and functions, each office may be organized differently. Grants and contracts filed in one office may be filed under the heading "state projects" in another. VIP correspondence in Senator A's office may be filed with his personal correspondence, while in Senator B's office it may be filed with her personal secretary's correspondence. Just as each congressperson deals with daily activities in a personal way, each office is administered in a personal and individual way.

Senate and House offices are governed by laws and procedures, of course. Laws govern the use of offices operating funds, use of franking privileges, campaign contributions, committee operating funds, and allocation of staff benefits, as well as many other financial functions. Where once there was great flexibility in the use of office operating funds, there is now tighter and more monitored control. Senate and House of Representatives staff manuals provide guidelines for filing financial reports, establishing staff responsibilities, using printing and franking privileges, and other activities.[5]

As each senator and representative comes into office for the first session he or she will hire staff members to organize the office. In most cases an administrative assistant or an office manager will be the person responsible for establishing the filing systems and functional divisions of the office. The most critical information necessary for determining records management and appraisal guidelines for a congressional office is the organizational structure. The archivist can use the written organizational structure to determine the original order of the files and also to establish a records management plan.

The "creator" of all files from a congressional office is considered to be the senator or representative. All staff in a congressperson's office work for him or her and therefore, their files are congressional files. Work done and files created by staff on the congressional payroll is work done for hire for the senator or representative. Personal files of a staff member such as those of professional organization activities must be sorted out from the congressional files.

The person responsible for establishing the filing system and organizational system for a congressional office must also be responsible for establishing a records management program. The *Records Management Handbook for United States Senators and Their Repositories* contains the established procedures for setting up a records management program for senatorial offices. The manual contains records management schedules for most senatorial office file categories, suggested deeds of gift or deposit agreements, information on utilizing the services of the National Archives records center, and other pertinent information and procedural guidelines. The Historical Office of the House of Representatives has issued "Guidelines for the Disposition of Members' Papers."[6] Repository archivists using the Senate *Records Management Handbook* and the House of Representatives papers disposal guidelines will have already dealt with most appraisal questions before the papers are received at the repository.

The *Congressional Papers Project Report* provides guidelines for archivists to use in evaluating congressional collections. Archivists should look for comprehensive coverage, ancillary files, uniqueness associated with the member, inclusion of background materials, documentation of committee activities, coverage of a long time span, and unsplit collections.

> Other minimum standards for congressional collections are ease of arrangement and description, appraisal and subsequent use, and preservation. The *Report* states that the following represent minimum quality: a collection's components are well defined and in good order; weedable series are easily distinguished; texts and indexes of automated files and system documentation exist, and automated formats are useable with the repository's technology; random papers files or microfilm are accessible through indexes or lists; nonpaper media items are identified, dated, indexed, and stored under archival conditions; and permanent files are on paper or other media of established quality.[7]

Appraisal Checklist

If the repository has determined that it will collect congressional papers it must also determine which collections are acceptable. Based on the collection development policy criteria for acceptance and the minimum standards for congressional collections in the *Report,* an appraisal checklist can be devised. A "no" response to more than 25% of the appraisal checklist questions would mark a collection as being one that the repository could not accept for preservation.

1. Is there a working records management plan for offices currently in operation?
2. Are any restrictions limited and reasonable?
3. Are the files complete for the congressional period and are pre- and post-congressional papers included?
4. Did the member of Congress serve a significant number of years and was he or she involved in events of historical importance that give the papers extensive research value?
5. Does system documentation along with texts and indexes exist for electronic records and can the records be accessed through the repository's computers or, are the files printed?
6. Have appropriate files been microfilmed, do indexes to the microfilm exist and is the film in good physical condition?
7. Are nonpaper media items identified, dated, indexed and in good physical condition?

If the collection comes from an office where there has been no records management plan in operation, then the following two questions must be asked along with questions 2 through 7:

8. Are the components of the papers well defined and in good order?
9. Are weedable series easily distinguished?

Discussion

1. Is there a working records management plan for offices currently in operation?

Repository archivists can make their jobs easier by working with congressional offices to establish records management programs while the member is in Congress. If an office does not have a records management program in place, the repository archivist can work with the House Historical Office or the Senate Archivist to create and implement records schedules.

Records management is essential to the preservation of members' papers. Participants at the Harper's Ferry Conference felt that "better records management practices in congressional offices is the most important activity that could be taken to improve the preservation of Congress' record. Yet the group seemed to feel that archivists have little influence over these practices."[8] While it is true that the impetus for better records management must come from within Congress, archivists can influence what happens. If repository archivists contact congressional offices at the beginning of congressional terms, an effective records management program can be developed. Repository archivists can also suggest that congressional staff archivists be hired to help institute records management practices.

Unfortunately, congressional staff members hesitate to devote any of their already limited time to records management unless it is made a priority by the senator or representative. Repository archivists can work with senior staff members from offices already committed to records management to pass the word of its value to other members of their state delegations. Then repository archivists can begin a campaign to provide information on records management to Washington staff as well as state office staff.

One of the major problems with appraising congressional papers is their enormous volume. Archivists may be able to review files in the senate office, the senate attic storage areas, the Suitland National Records Center, and in the state office, but almost never will all files be together in one place until they reach the repository. Therefore, archivists must review the major components of congressional collections and establish procedures for appraisal previous to receipt of a collection.

2. Only limited and reasonable restrictions are requested.

Many archivists will agree with the maxim that "no gift is ever free." Restrictions are one cost associated with manuscript collections. Members of Congress and their families may request that certain portions of personal materials be closed for a reasonable period of time due to sensitive information they contain. Other restrictions may be requested in order to protect living persons and to prevent libel. Limited time closures are acceptable but permanent restrictions should never be accepted by the repository. Archivists are faced with the requirements of the Federal Privacy Act and Freedom of Information Act which congressional offices usually adhere to even though the acts do not legally apply to the members' papers. Some congressional papers contain national security classified files which are restricted by statute. These must be declassified before being made available to researchers. Archivists should contact the Declassification Division of the National Archives and Records Administration regarding questions about such files. Copies of records of congressional committees are governed by

House and Senate rules. It is recommended that House committee records have restricted access for 30 years and Senate committee records for 20 years.[9]

3. The files are complete for the congressional period and pre- and post-congressional papers are included.

Completeness might mean that all the series from the congressional office that are appraised as permanent are included in the collection. For example, a set of congressional papers that did not include the personal correspondence between Members for the entire period the member was in Congress would not be considered complete. If senior staff members' papers, such as those of the administrative assistant, were missing, the papers would not be considered to be complete. Are party leadership files included for Members who held such offices as Majority Whip? Are campaign materials there? Other archivists might consider the files incomplete if photographs and copies of speeches were not included.

Members of Congress most often have pre- and post-congressional careers and activities. These files need to be collected to provide an overall history of the Member of Congress. Some people are elected to Congress after serving in state legislatures and other elected offices; or after a career in education, the legal profession, medicine, the military and recently homemaking. In the past, Members of Congress were farmers, merchants, and clergy before being elected to Congress. They may have gone back to the same work when their time in Congress ended. Throughout history some Members leave Congress when they are elected to higher office or appointed to other positions in the government. Today after leaving Congress many Members go back to their pre-congressional career and some start new careers such as lobbying. Pre-congressional work and activities can be a major influence on the Member's approach to congressional work, and life in Congress can affect a person's activities in a post-congressional career. Thus it is important that materials reflecting a Member's activities before entering Congress and after leaving be collected.

The pre- and post-congressional papers of a Member of Congress may by necessity be incomplete. Some Members of Congress go on to be appointed to presidential cabinet positions or are elected Vice-President or President. These papers will be wanted by the presidential libraries. Some congresspeople have served as governors or other state officials whose papers are by law designated for the state archives. The repository must determine if such splits in collections violate their collecting exclusions on split collections. Because so many congressional collections will have parts that are of interest to other types of repositories, cooperative collecting arrangements should be developed.

4. The Member of Congress served a significant number of years or was involved in events of historical importance that give the papers extensive research value.

What is the stature of the Member of Congress? Did he or she serve on or chair powerful congressional committees or did he or she serve as a leader in a political party? Was the Member ever elected or appointed to higher office or serve in state government executive positions? How many terms did the Member serve? If the Member served only one or two terms was he or she involved in legislation of historical significance that would increase the research value of the papers?

The Minnesota Historical Society has determined that it will not seek donor contracts with Members of the House of Representatives from Minnesota until after their first reelection. MHS's Congressional Papers Appraisal Committee has determined that those Representatives "who serve only one term are usually less historically important than those who serve several terms." Representatives who are defeated after one term will be contacted by the Society staff to request the donation of a very limited number of series. "In the case of a Representative who is defeated after one term, the acquisition staff will contact his/her office after the election, and request donation of a very limited number of series: mass mailings to constituents; biographical files; VIP correspondence; speech files; press releases; well organized newspaper clippings; and in some instances selected campaign files."[10]

Cynthia Pease Miller, Assistant Historian, U.S. House of Representatives, sees a need for archivists to rethink this appraisal guideline. She contends that:

> More members are coming to Congress at a younger age, and they are leaving at a younger age, especially from the House, to pursue other interests, run for other office, or accept appointment to other office. There are only 48 members of the present House with more than 20 years service (roughly 10%) and only 14 of those with 30 years service. If the present retirement/defeat rate continues, when the 104th Congress convenes in January 1995, more than half of the House will have been elected since 1990. This has serious implications for archivists and repositories interested in congressional papers. Foremost, it means there will be fewer "personalities," members with long service who may have been identified with certain issues.[11]

Stature may still be easier to judge than collection quality. The *Congressional Papers Project Report* recommends that archivists seek collections which document the roles for which the Member is deemed important. The roles should be evident in the entire collection. There must be quantity and quality as well as completeness and continuity.[12]

   5. Electronic records system documentation exists along with texts and indexes, and electronic records can be accessed through the repository's computer. Paper back-up systems exist for electronic records. (See Chapter 5 section on electronic records for more information.)

   Documentation, file codes, and other systems information are critical for understanding electronic systems used in congressional offices. The safest course for access is to have all computer files transferred to ASCII files or printed on paper. The Minnesota Historical Society considers these files so important that "efforts to both understand these systems and to appraise the data contained in them should take precedence over arrangements of the sampling, shipping, and acquisitioning of hundreds of cubic feet of case and issue files."[13] While not all archivists would agree with the Minnesota Historical Society's appraisal decision, most would agree that electronic records (machine readable records) have not eliminated paper files as once predicted. But they have made the archivist's job more difficult, especially with congressional papers. In recent years, the problem of the verbal nature of Congress has taken a new turn. While it is true that phone calls may not be documented, it is also true that electronic mail is not being saved on back-up disks nor printed out on paper. As with any electronic mail system, much of the "conversation" is trivial but, in Congress, staff members as well as senators and representatives may be transmitting substantial policy and decision making information across the electronic highway. Archivists must take care to collect such electronic mail.

   The *Records Management Handbook for United States Senators* reviews electronic records systems in the United States Senate up to 1992, and the House Information System issues guidelines useful to House offices. However, in 1993 the Internet came to Washington, D.C., and even the White House can be corresponded with by electronic mail, as can the Library of Congress and staff members in the Congress. It is still unclear how many senators and representatives are using the Internet, the electronic mail systems in their offices, and electronic mail among colleagues. Another concern that will need to be addressed is what electronic publications are staff receiving and can they be downloaded to individual disks or printed out for archival appraisal?

   Not only is the recent advent of electronic mail a difficulty, but the varying systems used in Congress create continuing archival problems. The first edition of the *Records Management Handbook for Senators* (1985) is help-ful in understanding some of the older computer systems used in the Sen-ate. For a basic background on the problems inherent in electronic records, see the standard by Margaret L. Hedstorm, *Archives and Manuscripts: Machine-Readable Records* (Chicago: SAA, 1984). Although the work needs updating, Hedstorm's publication is educational reading for archivists. Important for review also is the National Archives and Records Adminis-tration's *Strategic Plan for Information Systems and Technology, Fiscal Years 1991–1995* (published 1990) and other NARA guidelines on electronic records.

6. Appropriate files have been microfilmed and the microfilm is indexed and in good physical condition.

Files such as computer-generated cumulative indexes and reports should be preserved on computer output microfilm (COM). Clippings should also be microfilmed. The Senate microfilm office attempts to provide the Mem-bers' offices with archival quality microfilm. Offices, however, must develop and provide the access systems. Records management programs in the offices should incorporate guidelines for microfilm. To be useable, the microfilm must be kept in proper storage conditions or irreversible deterioration will begin. When possible the repository should also acquire the negative microfilm.

The repository must also be concerned about the equipment required to access the microfilm when it is received. Some offices still have their microfilm placed on cassettes and not on reels. These cassettes require specific types of microfilm readers that archival repositories do not always own.

7. Nonpaper media items are identified, dated, indexed and in good phys-ical condition.

Photographs, slides, videotapes, films, and audio tapes require proper storage in order to survive. Access to these items is impossible without proper labeling and indexing. Many repositories will not accept these materials unless they are completely identified. Other archivists contend that pho-tographs from congressional offices are worth the work to identify. James Edward Cross argues that point in his 1988 article, "The Science of Deduc-tion: Dating and Identifying Photographs in Twentieth Century Political Collections," and presents methods for such identification.[14] The simpler solution is to work carefully with congressional staff to make sure materials in the press files are identified and to follow established records schedules developed for the congressional office.

The criteria for past members whose papers are post–1950 and for past members whose files are pre–1950 list two points not included in the criteria for current members.

8. Are the components well defined and in good order?

9. Are weedable series easily distinguished?

Because the files of former members will usually be found in less than ideal storage conditions, archivists must review their collectability carefully. Physical condition could be very poor and all series could be mixed together with file labels missing. Of course, archivists deal daily with manuscript collections whose original order is lost, but the most valuable are those in which some of the original order can be reconstructed. This applies to congressional papers as well. Even when files are received from an office with no records management plan in place, following guidelines for appraisal in the *Records Management Handbook*, the House "Guidelines," will make the job possible to complete.

New Approaches to Appraisal and Collecting of Congressional Papers

Aronsson feels that standard archival practices and theories do not accommodate the special problems presented by congressional papers. The traditional archival procedures that encourage repositories to retain massive amounts of duplicate and probably minimally historically valuable materials must be rethought. The integrity of all collections, including congressional papers, must be maintained "but the meaning of integrity must be reevaluated if repositories are going to continue to acquire collections that typically exceed one thousand cubic feet and contain large quantities of non-unique materials." Can archivists appraise several congressional collections simultaneously to eliminate overlapping and duplicate files and still respect provenance? Aronsson believes they can.

She feels that many of the problems associated with congressional papers are caused by their size; therefore appraisal strategies should be developed to shrink them. Of course, archivists typically weed files, but according to Aronsson, in collections of congressional papers they weed only the things that are "generally acknowledged to have little historical significance, such as routine housekeeping records, duplicates, and published information." She states that many series within congressional collections are usually duplicated in the offices of other members serving at the same time. Duplication exists across party, district and state lines. The amount of duplication and the subsequent large collections it causes are unusable by researchers who cringe at the size, and unmanageable for repositories in terms of staff, space and financial cost. Strategies must be developed that "permit archivists to appraise (weed) these collections at some level of detail between that of the collection and the item."[15]

Aronsson proposes regional or state repositories where large numbers of congressional collections are appraised and processed simultaneously with archivists eliminating duplicate files while maintaining provenance for each collection.

The managers of the congressional collections in the Louisiana and Lower Mississippi Valley Collections (LLMVC) of the Louisiana State University Libraries have adapted Aronsson's suggestions and modified them to cover the state delegation. For post–1950 congressional papers the archivists seek to eliminate duplication in the files. They use a sliding scale so that there is a complete file of senatorial papers series for at least one Louisiana senator, usually the senior senator, for every year since 1948, when Russell B. Long first entered Congress. Long's papers have been fully processed for his entire congressional career. Legislative files, grant or project files, agency or department files, and state affairs files have been processed at the folder level. J. Bennett Johnston became a senator in 1973. The same series in Johnston's files were reviewed to determine duplications with Long's files and the duplicates were eliminated. Johnston's files after 1987 in these series will be fully processed as will all of his files in these series until the end of his time in the Senate in 1996. John Breaux became a senator in 1987. If his papers come to LLMVC, any files that duplicate Johnston's will be tossed until he becomes the senior senator in 1997. Files in these series within Louisiana representatives' papers that duplicate the senator's files will be eliminated. Series that reflect the individual's unique perspective will be appraised individually.

The Minnesota Historical Society (MHS) also seeks to document their entire state delegation, because "it has embraced the idea that the group of individuals representing the state in Washington is more than the sum of its parts. These collections are important both as pieces of a national collection documenting Congress as a whole, and as resources for more local study: the lives and attitudes of individual elected officials; the interaction (political and personal) of the state delegation; the local (district, state, and regional) issues and concerns which formed the crucible of national action."[16]

However, they will no longer accept all papers created by all congressional offices. The Congressional Papers Appraisal Committee feels that MHS does not have the resources to continue to acquire, arrange, and store these papers the way it did in the past and that the ever increasing bulk of such collections calls for new appraisal guidelines. The central goal of their guidelines is "to balance the Society's resources against the increasing bulk of Congressional collections, and to define the most stringent appraisal criteria possible, consistent with preserving collections which serve the long-term historical objectives of historians and other researchers." The Committee agrees with Aronsson that issues and projects dealt with among members of a state delegation can be redundant and the files duplicated.

The MHS will treat the papers of senators differently from representatives' papers for they feel that by documenting the activities of Minnesota senators more thoroughly than representatives they can receive "materials documenting concerns of importance from all corners of the state. The papers of Representatives, therefore, can be reduced further (especially such series as constituent correspondence), and focused to provide better documentation of those activities unique to the particular legislator and/or to his/her district."[17]

Such procedures will reduce the amount of "time and storage space the Society spends dealing with series such as case files and constituent correspondence." Staff time can then be focused on

> the files of administrative and legislative assistants, and on electronic records in the Congressional offices — records of indisputable long-term historical value but which have heretofore been acquired only sporadically if at all. Congressional staff tend to view their files as personal, and to overcome this tendency the Society must take pains to highlight these records and speak specifically to the respective staff members. Other series the acquisition staff will be seeking to highlight with Congressional staffs are those dealing with the member's party activities and his/her involvement with Congressional Membership Organizations.[18]

Aronsson warns, however, that new appraisal strategies require "meticulous background work." She believes that only by becoming extremely familiar with the work of the Congress, the individual senator or representative, the member's office, and the issues important to the member and her constituents can archivists be sure their appraisal decisions are valid. Archivists need the support and assistance of congressional staff and must gain such support while the member is still in Congress.[19]

Specific Recommendations for Appraisal

Paul in the *Records Management Handbook* has divided congressional papers collections into five subgroups: Personal/Political/Official Files, Legislative Files, Constituent Services Files, Press Relations/Media Activities Files, and Office Administration Files.[20] For each of these divisions Paul gives appraisal guidelines in the form of records schedules. Since the publication of the *Records Management Handbook,* the House of Representatives Historical Office has issued "Guidelines for the Disposition of Members' Papers." Recommendations from these two publications, from the Minnesota Historical Society's Division of Library and Archives, "Report of the Congressional Papers Appraisal Committee; *The Documentation of Congress*; and the practices of the Louisiana and Lower Mississippi Valley Collections are drawn together in this section as suggestions for possible appraisals of congressional papers. Few further comments to those in the *Handbook* and House "Guidelines" are needed for most series. Others, however, require more clarification. Each repository will, of course, find it necessary to adapt recommendations to their own circumstances.

Personal/Political/Official Files Subgroup

Archival series: appointment books, biographical, campaign caucus/political, chronological, daily schedules, diaries, financial disclosure reports, members' correspondence, memos of phone conversations/summaries, party leadership/congressional membership organizations, polling data, scrapbooks, trip files, VIP appointments/judgeships, and VIP correspondence.

Non-archival series: invitations, memorabilia, non-VIP appointment and correspondence, and telephone message slips.

"Personal files are valuable for the insights they provide about the member's activities while an elected official. The personal files reflect the senator's or representative's lifestyle and ways of interacting with cohorts, and they contribute to a researcher's understanding of the senator or representative as a person."[21]

Invitations are one series that continues to elicit appraisal debate among archivists. Aronsson feels that accepted ones merit attention by the archivist because "they reveal the activities of an individual member of Congress and also may help a researcher identify categories of social events attended by high-level federal officials." Paul also lists accepted invitations as a permanent series. But the Minnesota Historical Society disagrees that accepted invitations are archival because they are redundant. They feel the information is available in much more condensed form in the schedule files. MHS will retain accepted invitations if and when speech files are integrated into them. House guidelines state that accepted invitations should be retained only if they are part of a schedule or trip files. The user survey in *The Documentation of Congress* found that invitations were one of the series least used by researchers. At the LLMVC, accepted invitations files will be retained only if the information they contain is not duplicated in schedule, appointment, calendar, trip or correspondence files. When the information is duplicated elsewhere, the files will be sampled to retain the flavor of the activities associated with such files.

Archivists should remain aware that although they appraise personal files as permanent they may be hard to acquire. Many personal secretaries are very protective of the member they work for and see personal office files as private. Also, in some cases members will wish to retain some files from their personal offices when they leave Congress. It is important that repository archivists work with staff and members to insure that files appraised as permanent do eventually come to the archives.[22]

Legislative Files Subgroup

Archival: Bills authored/coauthored by member, briefing books, committee files, legislative assistants' files, staff project files, voting and attendance records.

Non-archival: bound volumes of the *Congressional Record* and duplicate files.

Most archivists agree that these are some of the most important of congressional papers, especially legislative assistants' (LAs) files which hopefully document the member's "participation in the introduction and movement of bills, his/her general legislative interest, impact, and influence, as well as the interaction of legislative concerns and interest with the pressures of his/her constituency. These files should document the development of policy positions and legislative initiatives by the legislative staff."[23]

Aronsson describes the job of legislative assistants as monitoring legislation and advising their bosses about all legislation occurring in Congress. Some legislative assistants who are experts in their fields of responsibility may even suggest possible legislative initiatives to members. Because of their involvement with legislation, their various responsibilities and their expertise in subject areas, legislative assistants' files are likely to be the most substantive in a member's office. Aronsson advises that archivists keep entire LA files unless they can process them item by item. Also she warns archivists to use caution in discarding the published materials found in LA files because such publications may be rare and not widely distributed elsewhere.[24]

LAs tend to keep extensive files but also tend to view the files as personal and not part of the member's papers. Archivists need to educate legislative assistants regarding the archival preservation of their files. Essentially LAs' files fall under the concept of "work for hire." They work for the member and would not be creating files regarding that work if they were not employed by the member. Therefore, files created during a LA's work-related activities are office files and part of the member's papers. LAs should not take their files with them when they change jobs or when the member leaves Congress. If the member permits, LAs may make copies of their files.

Connell B. Gallagher, in his article "A Repository Archivist on Capitol Hill" warns, however, that LAs may insist that their files are private to them and do not belong in the member's papers because they document confidential maneuvering by the LAs. Again, archivists must educate members of Congress and their staffs regarding archival preservation. Gallagher also discovered one administrative assistant who maintained that some LAs files represented opinions that were not always the same as the member whom the LA worked for. The archivist agreed to identify the LA files in this case as "an advisory satellite series."[25]

Committee files require careful attention. The House of Representatives "Guidelines" state that

> official records of the committee are maintained by the committee and, as part of the official records of the House of Representatives, are transferred to the Clerk of the House at the close of each Congress. It is unlikely that any will be found in a member's office files, but committee related materials in the offices of committee and subcommittee chairmen should be reviewed carefully and any official committee papers returned to the Clerk of the House.[26]

However, some original committee files will make their way to the repository in members' papers as will copies of items from the official files. Repository archivists need to carefully review these files during appraisal to remove and return to Congress any original, official committee files.

Materials that should be appraised for retention from committee files are unpublished hearings, copies of official files, annotated announcements, notes and correspondence.

In Congress there is often switching of staff members from committee assignments to assignments as legislative assistants. This creates confusion for archivists between committee files and staff files. For example, Gallagher dealt with one office where the senator had legislative assistants with responsibilities for three committees. He also had fourteen minority committee staff reporting to him (see *The Documentation of Congress* for information on how committees work). In the same office a minority subcommittee staff director also functioned as the senator's legislative assistant for education. "All of the records relating to education were interfiled with the official records of the subcommittee." The administrative assistant considered the subcommittee records to be part of the senator's personal papers so when the collection came to the repository, subcommittee records were included. The repository must now carefully weed for any official committee files and return them to Washington. "This blending of responsibilities is very common in Congress, and senators typically move staff from the personal office to the committee payroll at will." Such movement creates confusion in files. If microfilm exists of committee files, the microfilm can be ordered for the repository for researchers to review in order to alleviate some confusion.[27]

Constituent Services Subgroup

Archival: administrative assistants' files, grants and projects files (retain if on microfilm; if not, sample), state/district files (retain if on microfilm; if not, sample), agency/department files (retain if on microfilm; if not, sample), case work and issue files that affect legislation or that are of special interest to the member, case work and issue mail reports and indexes, grants and projects reports and indexes, state/district files reports and indexes, agency/department files reports and indexes, issue mail master library or library of form paragraph, and academy appointment registers.

Non-archival: case work and issue files of a routine nature, academy files, and others that should be sampled.

Constituent services files are items that "document the structure, management, and constituent service activities of the office; the role of the staff and their interrelationships; and their role in accomplishing ... goals."[28]

Files of the administrative assistant (AA) are categorized as part of constituent files. Administrative assistants who may have management and legislative responsibilities are usually the senior staff persons in a congressional office. Much of the work they do is confidential and sensitive. Therefore, they create few paper files except those for the most routine office management responsibilities. Some AAs can also have responsibilities for other areas such as military appointments. Aronsson states:

The administrative assistant's files should be preserved in their entirety. This person plays such an important role in the congressional office that his activities should be documented as fully as possible. Although a moderate amount of this material may not merit preservation, the end result of weeding the files does not justify the amount of time this task would require, particularly because this series is likely to be the smallest in the entire collection.[29]

Occasionally administrative assistants do maintain files. They require written reports and summary documents from the legislative assistants and other office staff as well as requiring written goals and objectives and strategic plans.[30] To find such files in a collection of congressional papers would be ideal. Hopefully, by working with administrative assistants, archivists can encourage the retention of thorough documentation.

Grants and projects files document the efforts of Members of Congress to funnel federal money to their home states and districts. Such activities may also be documented in agency or department files and state or district files. Such activities require a great deal of staff time and involvement. Paul suggests that it is easier to access and dispose of these files if they are kept separate from case work and issue files, even when they are managed by the same computer-based system.[31] Like legislative files these may contain near-print and privately printed materials that must be reviewed before being tossed. Any staff project file guides need to be retained as keys to the files and, when possible, computer reports and indexes for these files should be generated on computer output microfilm (COM). The COM should be retained; the paper files should not. If paper files are appraised for retention by the repository, the archivist should review them in the future for further weeding.

In academy files, any registers of applicants and appointees should be kept. Because of privacy concerns, many congressional offices now refuse to transfer academy files to repositories. Also, the information in these files is maintained by the academies. Unless the member maintains a close relationship with the appointees, there is no historical purpose in keeping the files.

Before the publication of the *Records Management Handbook for Senators* in 1985, many offices relied on the recommendations in the National Archives and Records Service's Office of Records Management, *Files Handbook for Congressional Offices*, which suggested central files.[32] However, the *Records Management Handbook* does not recommend central files and few current offices maintain "central files."

However, when an office has a central files system, legislative assistants may keep research and pending files at their desk with all correspondence and memos kept in the central files. Administrative staff, except the administrative assistant, will probably all file their materials in the central files. Appraising a "central files" series is difficult for it may be arranged alphabetically by topic. If the topics include "casework," "issues," "academy files," "grants or projects," etc., appraisal can follow the guidelines established for those series. Cross-references can be created in the repository to lead researchers to series within the central files.[33]

Case files are requests for help from constituents. Usually these cases are personal problems relating to federal agencies. Congressional offices devote large amounts of staff time to these cases but most archivists agree that they have little historical significance. Recent House of Representatives' "Guidelines" state that members are now refusing to transfer case files to repositories because of privacy concerns. The House "Guidelines" do, however, recommend that case files can "reflect a broader political importance (such as black lung disease, asbestos claims, toxic waste dumps). If filed topically, these may be sampled or statistically described as time and space allow."[34] Paul also recommends that cases which result in legislative initiatives or rule changes should be permanent, as should cases that are of particular importance to the member's state.[35] Some repositories do wish to keep case files and, if so, they should be sampled but sealed for a number of years to protect privacy. Congressional offices may microfilm case files and produce computer-generated name and subject indexes and statistical reports. If the microfilm is keyed to the indexes, keep the film. If the microfilm is not keyed to indexes, it may not be useable by researchers. Indexes, statistical reports, and summary sheets should be retained.

At the Louisiana and Lower Mississippi Valley Collections, case files of senators will be reviewed for retention of cases that lead to changes in legislation or which are of special interest to the senator and to Louisiana. Such cases are those involved with wetlands, oil and gas industry concerns, the environment, flood control, and other Louisiana interests as may arise in the future. This necessitates monitoring of the social and political concerns of Louisiana citizens which, of course, is one of the responsibilities of collecting for a "Louisiana" collection. Other cases, including those from representatives offices, are appraised as non-permanent and will be tossed. Cases retained will be closed for 75 years.

Many congressional repositories have in the past accepted vast quantities of case and issue files from members of Congress. Most of these have never been processed because of the time and expense involved. Most repositories will determine whether or not they must discard, sample, or maintain massive files in their entirety based on storage space, staffing and cost.

But caution is necessary for preventing the elimination of potentially valuable research files.

Each congressional office creates a tremendous volume of issue mail. Most issue mail is answered by computer generated form letter and it is important to retain master files of form paragraphs and a file of superseded paragraphs. All such items should be dated. Do not retain issue mail microfilm unless it is keyed to an index. Some issue mail will appear in legislative, agency or department files. Files that concern issues of particular significance to the member or to the state should be retained permanently. Other issue mail can be reviewed for sampling.

The Louisiana and Lower Mississippi Valley Collections will permanently retain the Issue Mail Master Library/Library of Form Paragraphs for senators' and representatives' offices. Issue Mail Indexes and Reports are also permanent for all offices. Issue mail from senators' offices will be carefully reviewed for possible sampling. Issue mail from representatives' offices will be randomly sampled.

Public Relations/Media Activities Files Subgroup

Archival: constituent newsletters or other mailings, editorials written by senator, newsletters, updates, identified photographs, press releases, speeches, identified audio and video tapes, identified films, media activities plans, newsletters, newspaper clippings about the member (one copy), press mailing lists (electronic or microfilmed), and press staff correspondence.

Non-archival: unidentified photographs, audio and video tapes, and films; paper copies of press mailing lists; duplicate copies of clippings or unorganized clippings; and any other duplicates.

"Press files provide valuable information about the attitudes and opinions of the senator or representative and should be kept in their entirety. Archivists probably should not refolder this material, however, because of the wealth of information found on the folder labels."[36] While this statement may be true for speech files, editorials, constituent mailings, newsletters, and press releases, other categories of press files need closer scrutiny.

Clippings are viewed by some congressional staff members as the essence of history — archivists have different views. Undated clippings lend little to historical research and background clippings in research files can be discarded. The redundant copies from clipping services can also be discarded. If clippings are retained they should be photocopied, scanned or microfilmed. More difficulty arises with the appraisal of nonprint materials such as photographs, audio tapes, video tapes and films. If photographs are identified they should be retained and the negatives acquired from congressional photographers. Aronsson summarizes:

> Photographs, like newsclippings, sometimes present more problems than they seem to be worth. Senators and representatives pose for photographs with almost every tour group from their home state, and their offices often keep file copies. Only the most organized offices label these photographs; others simply file them. The photographs' historical value is negligible, particularly when they are not identified. However, even the identified group shots reveal little information. Some photographs, though, may be historically significant — candid shots of the member's official travels, her personal photographs, and shots of the senator or representative in action. Such photographs are often difficult to locate, however. Those sent in by friends and admirers may be filed in the office's main filing system. The archivist must decide how much time to spend searching for them, keeping in mind that public officials are accustomed to being photographed and even the most casual shot may be totally contrived. Although photographs found in congressional collections may not be intrinsically valuable, they can enhance exhibits and are useful as illustrations in publications. Archivists must carefully evaluate their repositories' interest in photographs before deciding whether to keep them.[37]

Audio tapes are usually on cassette tapes or reel-to-reel tapes. Even if they are not labeled, archivists can listen to them to determine if the tape is identifiable and archival. Some audio recording materials, however, are no longer playable because equipment does not exist. If the repository wishes to retain such nonplayable items they must determine if they can afford the cost of transferring the audio to cassette or reel-to-reel tape. If the "dictabelt" or radio disk is identified and contains a historical speech, such as Huey P. Long's "Share the Wealth" speech, the cost of preservation is worth it. Otherwise the funds are best spent on other projects. The same is true of older video tapes and films. In the Russell B. Long Collection there are numerous such items that the LLMVC has decided to retain in the hopes of transferring them to VHS tape in the future. Each repository must carefully weigh the value of retaining these materials.

Office Administration Files Subgroup

Archival: Lists of current and former staff, office policy manuals and memos, trip files, operation manuals, file keys, staff meeting minutes, records management manuals, master library of form letters, support files for automated records and personnel manuals.

Non-archival: "Tickler" files, duplicate copies of memos, Library of Congress Loan Division files, job applications, security clearance files, parking files, office space and office equipment files, financial files for the office, and routine travel files.

While few of the office administration files are archival, some should be more carefully reviewed than others. File keys, support files for automated records, and staff lists will make the job of the archivists simpler. File keys (codes) should be kept — current and superseded. They could eliminate inappropriate rearrangement by repository archivists. Like staff lists, file keys may be hidden in the office managers' files, the personal secretaries' files, or the administrative assistants' files. If possible the archivist should request a copy of all file keys from sitting members. Staff lists are important for interpreting who handled what files, especially legislative files. Researchers will find these invaluable.

Repository archivists faced with enormous volumes of congressional papers need to critically rethink the appraisal of many series within the papers. After appraisal is completed, a congressional papers collection will retain some of the following types of records or files which require archival arrangement, preservation, and description[38]:

Personal/Political/Official (may include)
- appointment books, daily schedules, desk calendars
- personal diaries, journals
- personal secretaries' files
- correspondence: VIP, other members
- telephone logs, memos, summary sheets, reports
- biographical files
- scrapbooks, clippings files, microfilm of these
- invitations
- campaign/political party leadership/causes files
- chronological files
- financial disclosure reports/other financial
- VIP appointments/judgeships appointments
- trip files
- subject/topical files

Legislative Files (may include)
- "bill files": authored, coauthored, other
- briefing books
- legislative assistants' files

• legislative subject (topical) files and background research-voting and attendance records
  • committee files
  • staff project files
  • congressional record inserts
  • administrative assistant files
  • subject/topical/special interest to member of congress

Constituent Services
  • administrative assistants' files
  • casework
  • grants/projects
  • issue mail
  • library of form replies
  • statistical reports/indexes/summaries
  • departments and agencies
  • state affairs
  • military academy appointment
  • central files

Press Relations/Media Activities
  • press secretary's files
  • newsletters
  • clippings
  • editorials/columns
  • press releases
  • specialized or constituent mailings
  • speeches
  • photographs
  • TV and radio recordings, films, video
  • subject or research files

Office Administration
  • staff: lists of current and former staff, minutes of staff meetings, staff directories
  • manuals: files, personnel, operations, records management
  • travel files
  • policy memos
  • form letters library/indexes
  • procedures memos

The following sections discuss the detailed arrangement and description of the above series.

NOTES

1. Lewis J. Bellardo and Lynn Lady Bellardo, *A Glossary for Archivists, Manuscript Curators, and Records Managers* (Chicago: Society of American Archivists, 1992), 2, 29.

2. Paul, *Documentation of Congress*, 2–3.

3. Aronsson, "Appraisal," 81.

4. Connell B. Gallagher, "A Repository Archivist on Capitol Hill," *The Midwestern Archivist* 16, 1 (1991): 51.

5. United States Senate, *Senate Manual*, S. Doc. 98-1 (Washington: Government Printing Office, 1994), and United States House of Representatives, *Rules of the House of Representatives* (Washington: Government Printing Office, 1990).

6. Paul, *Records Management Handbook*; and Miller, "Guidelines."

7. Phillips, "Harper's Ferry Revisited," 32–33.

8. Mackaman, *Congressional Papers Project Report*, 23.

9. See Rules XI and XXXVI of the Rules of the House of Representatives, and Senate Rules XI and XXVI 10 (a), and S. Res. 474, 96th Congress; for an excellent discussion of access and restrictions see "Determining Access Policies," in Mary Jo Pugh, *Providing Reference Services for Archives and Manuscripts* (Chicago: Society of American Archivists, 1992), 55–59; for a discussion of legal concerns see Gary M. Peterson and Trudy Huskamp Peterson, *Archives & Manuscripts Law* (Chicago: Society of American Archivists, 1985).

10. Minnesota Historical Society, Division of Library and Archives, "Report of the Congressional Papers Appraisal Committee," 1993, 8; Mark A. Greene, "Appraisal of Congressional Records at the Minnesota Historical Society: A Case Study." *Archival Issues* 19 (Winter 1994): 31–43.

11. Cynthia Pease Miller to the author, March 23, 1994.

12. Phillips, "Harper's Ferry Revisited," 30.

13. Minnesota, "Report, Appraisal Committee," 4.

14. James Edward Cross, "The Science of Deduction: Dating and Identifying Photographs in 20th Century Political Collections," *Provenance* 6 (Spring 1988): 45–59.

15. Aronsson, "Appraisal," 83–84.

16. Minnesota, "Report, Appraisal Committee," 1.

17. *Ibid.*, 2.

18. *Ibid.*, 4.

19. Aronsson, "Appraisal," 82–84.

20. Paul, *Records Management Handbook*, v, 19–41.

21. Aronsson, "Appraisal," 90.

22. Gallagher, "A Repository Archivist," 53.

23. Paul, *Records Management Handbook*, 27.

24. Aronsson, "Appraisal," 87–88.

25. Gallagher, "A Repository Archivist," 55.

26. Miller, "Guidelines," 3–4.

27. Gallagher, "A Repository Archivist," 52–53.

28. Paul, *Records Management Handbook*, 29.

29. Aronsson, "Appraisal," 87.
30. Gallagher, "A Repository Archivist," 56.
31. Paul, *Records Management Handbook*, 31.
32. For example, Senator Sam Nunn's files from 1972–1978 were arranged in one central file, Naomi L. Nelson to the author, April 18, 1994. Some offices however still institute central files. From 1948–1978 Senator Russell B. Long's files were decentralized and the system of central files put in place in 1979.
33. See the example of series descriptions for central files on page 78. Gallagher states that Senator Stafford's office had a central office file that included series entitled "Blue Slips" (copies of all letters sent, 35 feet); "Federal Government" (files of contacts with the Executive branch, 56 feet); "Committees" (83 feet); "Cases" (51 feet); "General Subjects" (33 feet); "Acknowledgments" (7 feet); "Requests" (20 feet); "Robos" (form letters, 19 feet); and "Vermont Issues" (29 feet). These centralized files were arranged alphabetically by topic for each session of Congress, and they received a preliminary weeding in Washington during the packing process. The "Blue Slips" series had little intrinsic value because it was a duplicate file and because the contents were repetitive. Still, it has some "slice of life" value as a record of every outgoing letter. This file was microfilmed and the originals were destroyed. These were onion skin and it took two months to prepare the 35 feet of them for microfilming as all preparation for filming must be provided by the office, not the Senate microfilm department. This was not a profitable use of time, so we abandoned earlier plans to film 17 feet of clippings and the large casework file. Members really need to use microfilm as a records management tool over the long term; it is impossible to do much in a few months." Gallagher, "A Repository Archivist," 54.
34. Miller, "Guidelines," 3.
35. Paul, *Records Management Handbook*, 29.
36. Aronsson, "Appraisal," 89.
37. *Ibid.*, 94–95.
38. This list is adapted from Paul, *Records Management Handbook*.

CHAPTER 3

Arranging and Describing Congressional Papers

Each member of Congress is responsible for the on-site management of office files and determines the archival disposition of his or her personal papers and office files. Many members have placed their papers with libraries, historical societies or presidential libraries in their state. Today, almost 1,000 archival repositories in the United States preserve and provide access to congressional papers.

Findings in *The Documentation of Congress* show that:

> Individuals who use congressional collections find them to be the most valuable source of information for biographical and public policy studies, but many of the collections are difficult to use. Academic researchers seek improvements in access through better indexing, more detailed descriptions, standardization of finding aids, and microfilm publication of important sequences so that scholars may access them through interlibrary loan.[1]

Unfortunately, the variation among finding aids created by repositories makes congressional papers difficult for researchers to use. The descriptive terminology varies, as does the understanding among archivists of the legislative process.[2] Because of these variations, standardization in the arrangement and description of congressional papers is long overdue. Adherence by congressional offices to the guidelines for records management from the House and Senate Historical Offices has led to conformity in records management throughout Congress, which makes standardization in arrangement and description more plausible. This manual will assist congressional papers archivists in providing broader, easier and more standard access.

But before beginning processing, archivists should become familiar with the functions of Congress by reading *The Documentation of Congress*, and with the variety of record series that will be found, by reviewing the *Records Management Handbook for Senators and Their Archival Repositories* and the House of Representatives' "Guidelines for Disposition of Members' Papers." Congressional archivists should also study and use Frederic Miller's *Arranging and Describing Archives and Manuscripts* as their guide to the theory of processing and then apply that guidance to processing congressional papers.

Aronsson commented in 1984 that "most archivists treat the papers of senators or representatives as personal papers, processing them as they would process most manuscript collections. That is, they examine collections at the item level, discard little, and refolder most of the material. Processing such papers with a straight records approach, however, may not be any more appropriate."[3] Since that time, archivists have refined the arrangement and description of congressional papers into a blending of the two approaches mentioned by Aronsson. If a congressional office implements a proper records management plan, then the "files" tend to be handled by the repository in a more "records" orientation. If the congressional office does not have a proper records management plan, then the "files" tend to be handled more as personal "papers."

After appraisal, the steps in preparing — processing — a congressional papers collection for research use and historical preservation are accessioning, arrangement, preservation, and description. Appraisal, however, can continue to occur as needed during processing. Appraisal is defined and discussed in Chapter 2.

Accessioning

Usually, most appraisal takes places before the congressional collection comes to the repository. Once the collection is acquired and transferred to the archives, the next step is accessioning. Repositories should follow their standard procedures. Accession numbers should be assigned and accession forms completed with the appropriate information.

The purpose of accessioning is to gain basic physical and intellectual control over the collection. Accessioning is defined as: "1. The formal acceptance into custody of an acquisition, and 2. An acquisition so recorded."[4]

Figure 3.1 is an example of the "Accession Record" sheet from the Senator Richard B. Russell Memorial Library at the University of Georgia Libraries. Intellectual control is gained by completing an accession form with brief descriptive content notes and a preliminary inventory.[5] A preliminary inventory consists of a biography; a short description of each series that tells

Figure 3.1. Acession Record

RICHARD B. RUSSELL LIBRARY FOR POLITICAL RESEARCH AND STUDIES
The University of Georgia Libraries
ACCESSION RECORD

Accession Number:

Date Received: **by:**

Date Accessioned: **by:**

Title:

Addition to:

Donor/Source:

Address:

Deed of Gift: **Restrictions:**
        Copyright:

Arrival Status (How were records received?):

Description of Material (type, condition, arrangement, content of records):

Dates:

Quantity:

Location:

Reprinted with permission of the Richard B. Russell Library for Political Research and Studies

content, arrangement, years covered, and the number of boxes for that series; and an outline of what materials each box contains. The physical control gained at this level includes assigning an accession number, examining the existing arrangement, retaining the original boxes and folders but labeling them with source and accession number and identifying box contents.

Many times there is confusion between accessioning and processing. Accessioning, according to Miller in *Arranging and Describing Archives and Manuscripts*, is the time when the appropriate sets of records [series] are identified, not the time when the processing is actually completed. "Accessioning at all repositories commonly involves five related activities: 1) preparatory on-site work; 2) physical, legal, and administrative transfer; 3) physical records analysis; 4) content analysis; and 5) preliminary listing."[6] Archives with an active collecting program will always have delays between the time the collection is accessioned and the time when full processing begins. These processing backlogs can be very large or small and the delays several years long or only a period of a few months.

Miller states that during accessioning the collection should be identified by provenance or type of series. After such identification, physical and intellectual analyses can proceed. Although some congressional offices transfer files to a repository on a yearly basis, most do not transfer files until the office closes. Therefore, rather than accessioning congressional papers by type of series (as most records would be accessioned), they will be accessioned by provenance.

Within congressional papers, archivists may find groupings of current and past family members merged with those of the Member of Congress. The original order and filing structure will help determine whether or not separate collections should be established for various family members or just separate series. Sets of business and organizational records included in family papers may not be complete enough to be considered separate accessions.[7] With congressional papers the opposite may be true — the papers may contain complete files on the congressional aspect of the person's life but little on family and pre- and post-congressional careers. For example, the papers of Senator Mike Gravel at the University of Alaska–Fairbanks consist of the majority of the records created in the Senator's offices during his time in the Senate. However, no records of Gravel's real estate and business career before his election to the Senate nor any personal papers before or after his Senate career are included. In contrast, the papers of Senator Russell B. Long at Louisiana State University contain all Senate office files, pre- and post-congressional career files, and family materials.

Further weeding will need to take place during the accessioning of congressional collections. Even in the office with the most thorough records management practices, there will be some materials in the files that cannot be eliminated until the files are received in the repository. Weeding at this stage might simply involve removing duplicates.

Some basic preservation work should be accomplished during

preliminary processing. Archivists should separate items needing special housing such as audio and visual tapes, films, and electronic records. Also, stabilize housing by removing materials from boxes that are broken, damaged or inappropriate for the materials they contain.

Frequently, appraisal of a congressional papers collection cannot take place until the collection is received in the repository. This happens when the collection is acquired from the member's home or storage area after death. It also happens if the repository steps in to acquire a group of papers right before a member must vacate his or her Washington, D.C., office because of election defeat or in case of the member's death. When this occurs, appraisal and accessioning must take place at the same time.

Review of the Basic Principles of Arrangement and Description

The basic principles of arrangement and description are applied to congressional papers just as to other collections in a repository. To review, Miller explains the important differences between archives and manuscripts. "Archives are the non-current but still useful records of an organization or institution preserved by that organization or institution." Manuscript collections are materials "created or gathered by an organization or individual but transferred from the original custodian to a collecting repository, such as a local historical society or university library."[8] Therefore, using Miller's distinction, congressional papers are manuscript collections.

Miller states that processing — arrangement and description — is basically the simple ordering and listing of records. Theoretically, arrangement and description may be viewed as the archival equivalent of library classification and cataloging. The functions of arrangement and description are similar, but the end results and the underlying principles are different.[9]

The underlying principles of archival arrangement are *provenance* and *original order*. Provenance simply means the creator or source. Records maintained according to provenance are identified and kept together by source or creator rather than by a classification scheme. Common subjects in materials do not permit intermingling of those from different creators. Original order means that the files are retained in the internal arrangement imposed by their creator or source.[10]

The results of archival arrangement are the identifying and bringing together "sets [series] of records derived from a common source which have common characteristics and a common file structure and the identifying of relationships among such sets of records and between records and their creators." The results of archival description are to provide information about the "origin, context, and provenance of different sets of records, their filing structure, their form and content, their relationships with other records, and the ways in which they can be found and used."[11]

The underlying principle of archival description is one of collective description rather than individual description of single items (as in library description). The results of archival description are multiple page inventories and other narrative analysis, not a single catalog entry.

Arranging

INTELLECTUAL ARRANGEMENT

Arrangement is defined as:

> the intellectual and physical processes and results of organizing documents in accordance with accepted archival principles, particularly provenance, at as many as necessary of the following levels: repository, collection, record group or fonds, subgroup(s), series, subseries, file unit, and item. The processes usually include packing, labeling, and shelving and are primarily intended to achieve physical control over archival holdings.[12]

In 1964, Oliver W. Holmes detailed the five-level hierarchy of arrangement which archivists have so often applied to records and manuscripts. The five levels of control are repository, record group or manuscript collection, series, file unit, and document. This hierarchy requires every document be assigned to one file unit (such as a folder) every file to one series and every series to one office of origin.[13] The physical arrangement of archives begins at the series level and over the years the five-level model has been modified to fit actual practice by adding two other levels: subgroups (within record groups or collections) and subseries (within series). The number of subgroups and subseries can "in theory" be extended endlessly. However, the best arrangement is the minimum number of subgroups and subseries needed to make the records (papers) accessible. Provenance of record group, subgroup, or collection is an intellectual arrangement, not a physical one, and provides information about the records' (papers') creators. Physical grouping filing structure (series, subseries and files) provides information about the records (papers).[14]

These concepts apply to congressional papers as well. Subgroups most often are intellectual divisions as opposed to physical divisions. Intellectual division into subgroups by function in the arrangement of congressional papers helps to guide the researcher to the documents needed. It also helps the archivists as they arrange and describe collections.

As stated in the section on appraisal, knowing the functions of congressional offices will assist archivists in the proper arrangement and description of papers. In the *Records Management Handbook for Senators*, Paul establishes functional relationships among series of files within the office structure. Although every office is managed and divided hierarchically in its own individual scheme, all have the same basic functional responsibilities. The functions of a congressional office are legislative, representational, political, administrative, and external relations. The legislative function

> includes the formulation and passage of bills that become law, including revenue bills and appropriations measures; the "executive" function of providing advice and consent on nominations and treaties; the "judicial" function of impeachment; the oversight function; the investigative function; and the budgetary function. Representation includes activities designed to promote the views, goals and agendas of a constituency, providing constituent services, and communicating with one's constituency. Political functions are defined as establishing a leadership and an internal organization that facilitate priority setting, policy formulation, and consensus building. It includes campaigns, elections and the role of political parties. Administrative functions include the establishment of internal rules and operating procedures within each House, establishing ethical norms, establishing administrative and support offices and agencies, providing for the physical plant, and maintaining security. External relations includes a variety of activities deriving from Congress' extensive interaction with outside groups, institutions, and agencies. This function would include relations with executive and judicial branches, the media, lobbyists, and think tanks.[15]

Functional subgroups (intellectual divisions) created for congressional papers can be: Personal/Political/Official Files, Legislative Files, Constituent Services Files, Public Relations/Media Activities Files, and Office Administration Files. These divisions are based on the functions that take place in congressional offices. Series (physical divisions) come under functional subgroups. For example, one series under the Legislative function subgroup might be Legislative Assistants' files. This series could contain all types of individual documents: letters, memos, reports, telephone logs, notes, etc.

When dealing with family papers of a member of Congress, the archivist must determine whether or not those papers will be a separate collection (on the basis of a separate creator) or whether they should remain part (a subgroup) of the representative's papers. If a husband's files are integrated into and throughout the representative's papers they must stay as part of the representative's papers. The Louisiana and Lower Mississippi Valley Collections processed Carolyn Bason Long's papers as a separate collection rather than as a subgroup of Senator Russell B. Long's papers. Mrs. Long's papers had always been filed separately from any of the Senator's files and therefore could be handled as a separate collection by a separate creator. However, within Senator Long's files in correspondence, clippings, scrapbooks, and writings there were many items dealing with Huey P. Long, the Senator's father. Therefore, the Huey P. Long papers remained as a series within the family papers subgroup of Senator Long's collection.

Record and manuscript groups are arranged into series which is the commonly accepted central unit of most processing work. The series is defined as

> file units or documents arranged in accordance with a filing system or maintained as a unit because they result from the same accumulation or filing process, the same function, or the same activity, have a particular form (2), or because of some other relationship arising out of their creation, receipt, or use. A series is also known as a record series.[16]

A further descriptive breakdown can be the subseries: "a body of documents within a series readily identifiable in terms of filing arrangement, type, form, or content."[17] Documents are the individual items in a file unit (folder/title) within the series (subseries, etc.).

The determination of series and subseries in collections with good records management programs might require only the identification of filing groups established by the office. Subseries will also be recognizable filing units. There are two kinds of series. The first is based on alphabetically, chronologically, or geographically arranged records. In congressional papers such series could be correspondence, legislative files, press files, or bills files. The second is records filed together because of a common format [microform] or activity/function [committee files]. These series may include a mixture of documents types and filing arrangement.[18]

There are also two types of subseries. Subseries must be logical divisions of the series. The first type of subseries is created by the alphabetical or chronological division or part of a series such as letters sent and letters received. There might be two subseries under a member's Bills Files Series: those authored and those co-authored. These subseries are designated by virtue of the filing of the documents within the files. The second type occurs when files are "nested," such as an alphabetical arrangement of Agency Files. Files could be designated: A-D (subseries), Environmental Protection Agency (subseries), F-U (subseries), and Veterans' Affairs Administration (subseries). These two agencies may be designated subseries because of the large number of files the office kept on these two agencies. Such a filing structure shows that the member was heavily involved in activities regarding these two agencies.

The order of a series can be chronological — such as trip files or bills files — or alphabetical — such as case files or correspondence. A third order could be by a classification scheme used in the congressional office, such as central files. If a collection of papers is disorganized, the archivist may need to construct series and subseries according to types of documents or the function or activity represented by documents. With large congressional collections, archivists seldom do detailed arrangement below the folder level and are not concerned with the internal order of documents within folders. Some series, however (VIP correspondence, bills sponsored), will require item level arrangement. Both archivists and researchers must remember that when one series in a collection is arranged at the item level, it does not mean that all series will receive the same level of control.[19]

The following model of the Representative John Smith Papers inventory shows how subgroups, series and subseries can appear in the intellectual and physical arrangement of a group of congressional papers.

MODEL INVENTORY
   Group Representative John Smith Papers [provenance]
      Subgroup Personal/Political/Official Subgroup [intellectual division — functional]
         Series Appointment Series [physical division — filing of documents]
            Subseries Appointment books [physical division — type of document]
            Subseries Daily schedules/itinerary [physical division — type of document]
            Subseries Desk calendars [physical division — type of document]
         Series Diaries/Journals (personal) [physical division — type of document]
         Series Writings and manuscripts (personal) [physical division — type of document]
         Series Personal Secretaries [physical division — filing of documents]
            Subseries Financial disclosure reports [physical division — type of document]
            Subseries Trip files [physical division — filing of documents]
         Series Correspondence Series [physical division — type of document]
            Subseries VIP correspondence files [physical division — type of document]
            Subseries Alphabetical correspondence files [physical division — filing and type of documents]

Series Telephone Series [physical division — type of document]
> *Subseries* Telephone logs/memos [physical division — type of document]
> *Subseries* Summary sheets/reports [physical division — type of document]
> *Subseries* Telephone reports [physical division — type of document]

Series Scrapbooks/clippings [physical division — type of document]

Series Party leadership [physical division — filing of documents]

Series Caucus/political party [physical division — filing of documents]

Series Campaign committee [physical division — filing of documents]

Series Chronological [physical division — filing of documents]

Series Invitations [physical division — type of document]
> *Subseries* Accepted, A–Z [physical division — filing and type of documents]
> *Subseries* Declined, chronological [physical division — filing and type of documents]

Series Job recommendations/appointments [physical division — type of document]
> *Subseries* VIP appointments [physical division — type of document]
> *Subseries* Judgeships appointments [physical division — type of document]

Series Miscellaneous [physical division — filing of documents]
> *Subseries* Memorabilia [physical division — type of documents]

Subgroup Legislative [intellectual division — functional]

Series Subject (topical) and background research [physical division — filing of documents]

Series Bills [physical division — type of document]
> *Subseries* Authored [physical division — filing and type of documents]
> *Subseries* Coauthored [physical division — filing and type of documents]

Series Legislative Assistants' Files [physical division - filing of documents]

Series Staff projects [physical division — filing of documents]

Series Legislation of special interest to member [physical division —filing of documents]

Series Briefing books [physical division — type of document]

Series Voting/attendance records [physical division — type of document]

Series Committee files [physical division —filing of documents]

   Subseries Chair, Committee on XXX [physical division —filing of documents]

   Subseries Subcommittee files [physical division —filing of documents]

Series Congressional Record inserts [physical division — type of document]

Subgroup Constituent Services [intellectual division — functional]

Series Administrative Assistants' Files [physical division —filing of documents]

Series Casework [physical division —filing of documents]

   Subseries Casework staff files, A–Z, sampled [physical division —filing and type of documents]

   Subseries Casework reports and indexes (electronic records) [physical division — type of document]

Series Issue mail [physical division — type of document]

   Subseries Issue mail, sampled [physical division —filing and type of documents]

   Subseries Master library/library of form paragraphs [physical division — type of document]

   Subseries Issue mail reports and indexes (electronic records) [physical division — type of document]

Series Agency/department [physical division —filing of documents]

Series State/district [physical division —filing of documents]

Series Military Academy appointment [physical division — type of document]

   Subseries Appointments, A–Z [physical division — type of document]

   Subseries Summaries [physical division — type of document]

Subgroup Press Relations/Media Activities [intellectual division — functional]

   Series Press files series [physical division —filing of documents]

      Subseries Newsletters [physical division — type of document]

      Subseries Editorials/columns [physical division — type of document]

      Subseries Press releases [physical division — type of document]

      Subseries Specialized or constituent mailings [physical division — type of document]

      Subseries Subject or research files [physical division — filing of documents]

    Series Newspapers clippings/scrapbooks [physical division — type of document]

    Series Photographs [physical division — type of document]

    Series Recordings [physical division — type of document]

      Subseries Audio [physical division — type of document]

      Subseries Video [physical division — type of document]

      Subseries Film [physical division — type of document]

Subgroup Office Administration [intellectual division — functional]

    Series Central files [physical division — filing of documents]

    Series Staff information [physical division — filing of documents]

      Subseries Lists of current and former staff/directories [physical division — type of document]

      Subseries Minutes of staff meetings [physical division — type of document]

    Series Manuals [physical division — type of document]

      Subseries Records management manual [physical division — type of document]

      Subseries Personnel manual [physical division — type of document]

      Subseries Operations manual [physical division — type of document]

      Subseries Files manual [physical division — type of document]

      Subseries Policy and procedures manual [physical division — type of document]

    Series Memorandums: policy and procedures [physical division — type of document]

    Series Form letters library/indexes [physical division — type of document]

    Series Electronic systems documentation [physical division — type of document]

    Series Travel/trips [physical division — filing of documents]

Another intellectual arrangement might be to have only two subgroups: legislative and administrative. The files that detail the legislative function would stand alone as a subgroup of the congressional papers. All other functions: Personal/Political/Official, Constituent Services, Public Relations/Media Activities, and Office Administration will fall under the subgroup, Administrative. Gallagher describes such an organization with the papers of Vermont Senators Robert T. Stafford and Patrick J. Leahy in his article "A Repository Archivist on Capitol Hill."[20] The following model inventory shows such an arrangement.

MODEL INVENTORY
    Group Senator Helen Jones Papers [provenance]
      Subgroup Administrative [intellectual division — functional]
        Series Appointment files
        Series Diaries/Journals (personal)
        Series Writings and manuscripts (personal)
        Series Personal Secretaries
          Subseries Financial disclosure reports
          Subseries Trip files
        Series Correspondence files
        Series Telephone logs, memos, summary reports
        Series Scrapbooks/clippings
        Series Party leadership files
        Series Caucus/political party
        Series Campaign committee files
        Series Invitations
          Subseries Accepted, A–Z
          Subseries Declined, sampled
        Series Job recommendations/appointments
        Series Miscellaneous
        Series Administrative Assistants' files
        Series Casework
          Subseries Staff files, A–Z, sampled
          Subseries Reports/indexes (electronic)
        Series Issue mail
          Subseries Issue mail, sampled
          Subseries Master library form paragraphs
          Subseries Reports/indexes (electronic)
        Series Agency/department
        Series State/district

    Series Military academy appointments
    Series Press files
       Subseries Newsletters
       Subseries Press releases
    Series Newspapers clippings/scrapbooks
    Series Photographs
    Series Recordings, TV, radio, audio, video, films
    Series Central files
    Series Staff information
    Series Manuals
    Series Memos: policy/procedures
    Series Form letters library/indexes
    Series Electronic systems documentation
    Series Travel/trips
Subgroup Legislative [intellectual division — functional]
    Series Subject (topical) and background research
    Series Bills
       Subseries Authored
       Subseries Coauthored
    Series Legislative Assistants
    Series Staff projects
    Series Legislation of special interest to member
    Series Briefing books
    Series Voting/attendance
    Series Committee files
       Subseries Chair, Committee on XXX
       Subseries Subcommittee
    Series Congressional Record inserts

    Such an intellectual arrangement is acceptable, but a more extensive subgroup division will aid researchers and archivists in their work.

    Another example of intellectual and physical arrangement for a collection of congressional papers is the one used at the Louisiana and Lower Mississippi Valley Collections for the Senator Russell B. Long Collection. This arrangement maintains original order from the congressional office as much as possible. Because there were extensive family and pre-Senate career files with the Senate papers, the archivists chose to arrange them into two subgroups. These family and pre-Senate papers were dealt with as any group of family manuscripts. Senator Long now heads a private law firm and after his retirement a 6th series will be added to his collection representing his post-

Senate career. The repository will probably also receive other files which are Senate-related in the future. When received, such files will receive description in an addendum to the current finding aids and will physically be housed at the end of the current collection.

INVENTORY EXAMPLE
    Group Russell Billiu Long Collection
        Subgroup Long Family Papers [intellectual division]
            Series Huey Pierce Long Papers
            Series Earl Kemp Long Papers
            Series Family Papers
        Subgroup Russell Billiu Long Papers [intellectual division]
            Series RBL Early Years
                Subseries Personal Correspondence
                Subseries Louisiana State University Papers
                Subseries Naval Career Papers
                Subseries Business/Civic Papers
                Subseries Miscellaneous
            Series Executive Counsel to Earl Kemp Long Papers
            Series UNITED STATES SENATE
                Subseries Senate Office Files
                    Sub-subseries Personal Office Files
                    Sub-subseries Administrative Assistants
                    Sub-subseries Legislative Director
                    Sub-subseries Legislative Assistants
                    Sub-subseries Legislative Files
                        General Legislative Files
                        Bills Sponsored and Co-sponsored
                        Voting Record
                    Sub-subseries Department and Independent Agency Files
                    Sub-subseries Louisiana State Affairs
                    Sub-subseries U.S. Army Corps of Engineers
                        Projects Files
                    Sub-subseries Special Issue Files
                    Sub-subseries Automated Correspondence Systems Files
                    Sub-subseries Press Files
                        General Press Files
                        Press Secretary's files
                        Films, audio tapes and video tapes
                        Photographs

> Scrapbooks
>   *Subseries* Senate Committees
>   *Sub-subseries* Democratic Steering Committee
>   *Sub-subseries* Finance Committee
>   *Subseries* Senate Assistant Majority Leader Files
> *Series* Political Files
>   *Subseries* Senate Campaign Files
>   *Subseries* Democratic National Party and National Campaign Files
>   *Subseries* Louisiana Political Files
> *Series* Social
>   *Subseries* Mardi Gras Files
>   *Subseries* Other Social Occasions Files
>   *Subseries* Memorabilia

All intellectual and physical arrangement should be proceeded by the archivist's becoming familiar with the functions of Congress and the Member's work. The archivist must become knowledgeable about the Member of Congress, the legislation he or she was responsible for, the committees served on, the role played in party politics, state projects he or she supported, and the Member's personal history. Reading through scrapbooks and biographies as well as resumes aids in compiling this knowledge. The archivist's processing work will also be aided by information on the operations of the congressional office, the file systems, records management procedures, the names of office staff and their assignments, and documentation on electronic systems. Also useful are file headings, staff lists, and biographies.

Physical Arrangement

Working with congressional papers from offices with a records management plan is similar to working with "archives," while working with those from an office without a records management plan is closer to working with "personal papers."

This section is an overview of the physical arrangement of congressional papers. Chapter 4 gives detailed suggestions for the physical and intellectual arrangement of specific series found in congressional papers.

Most repositories have processing worksheets that are to be filled out as the processing staff completes the steps in the arrangement and description of a group of papers. (See Figure 3.2, "Processing Worksheet," Richard B.

Russell Library on Political Research and Studies, University of Georgia Libraries.) All repositories should have a procedures manual which deals with the specific steps to be taken in order to process congressional papers collections.[21]

Arrangement can be simply organizing files within a collection that is in excellent order or completely restructuring a collection that has lost all original order. Such disordered collections will need work at the series, folder and even document levels.

Archivists must realize that sometimes original order represents nothing but poor or incorrect filing by office workers. Such order may require rearrangement. The original order to be retained is that which documents the activity of the congressional office, not the caprices of file clerks.[22] Of course, that is not to say that archivists should change the order of files just for the sake of rearrangement. The papers of Edward James Gay, U.S. Senator from Louisiana 1918–1921, were rearranged from a combination alphabetical and chronological group to one of pure chronology with no series. While this was done in the days when archivists had little training and when "calendaring" was considered to be the accurate finding aid, losing the original order was wrong. While it may not have been a perfect filing system, the original order of Senator Gay's papers would have told researchers more about the Senator and would have aided their use of his papers.

One approach to filing problems in congressional papers and a possible solution is discussed in the introduction to the Frank Church Papers, Boise State University:

> After 24 years and countless files clerks, the Church Collection presented a distinct processing challenge. Many of the older files had been in storage in a Federal Record Center in Maryland. Others had been stored in the "attic" of the Senate Office Building. Much, of course, was in the active file in the Senator's office. How to organize all this paper was the question when processing began at Boise State. Since the Church office files were subject-oriented, it was decided to follow this arrangement and use a chronological sequence within each subject. One major problem was that over the years the file clerks gave differing interpretations to the same subject. Little effort was expended to reorganize misfiled information. The BSU processing staff determined to make the computer index the instrument of cohesion. Because index information was entered into the computer while processing was under way, it was not possible to number the boxes consecutively as is the general practice. By breaking the collection into series numbers the processing staff was able to enter the names, subjects and folder titles as each unit was processed (the database used is Q&A). The "General" section, which precedes more specific files in some parts of the Collection, seems to have been used by Church's staff to file miscellaneous material that did not fit into a more specific location. Letters coded

Figure 3.2. Processing Record

Richard B. Russell Library for Political Research and Studies
The University of Georgia Libraries

Processing Record

I. <u>Accession</u>

Collection Name:_____

Inclusive Dates:_____Accession Number:_____

Amount of Material:_____

Restrictions:_____

II. <u>Preliminary</u>

1. General Type of Material: (office files, personal papers, organizational papers, etc.)

2. Specific Type of Material: (clippings, correspondence, film, bound, photographs, published records, memorabilia, etc.)

3. Arrangement (alphabetical, chronological, numerical, grouped by subject)

4. Condition of records and conservation recommendations:

5. Major subjects:

6. Notes: (prominent person represented in correspondence, significant events, etc.)

"General" can include more than one issue, or can be on a single topic which never generated sufficient volume to need its own location. Because "General" includes such a wide variety of topics, researchers who wish an overview can consult these files first, then pursue more specific interests in the subject index and the subject areas of the files.[23]

During appraisal, repository archivists should determine which series are to be discarded, which ones are permanent, and which ones are to be

Figure 3.2. Processing Record (continued)

III. <u>Processing</u>

    Date   Initial

    _____   _____ Processing initiated
    _____   _____ Original order: maintained/established
    _____   _____ Preliminary inventory prepared
    _____   _____ Conservation of documents (surface cleaning)
    _____   _____ Folders replaced
    _____   _____ Materials repaired
    _____   _____ Fasteners replaced
    _____   _____ RBR identification seal used
    _____   _____ Duplicates removed
    _____   _____ Photocopied all clippings, thermofax
    _____   _____ Item count
    _____   _____ Box list completed
    _____   _____ Folder count
    _____   _____ Boxes and folders labeled
    _____   _____ Boxes shelved
    _____   _____ Finding aid completed

IV. <u>Remarks</u>

V.   <u>Unprocessed material (type and volume)</u>

Reprinted with permission of the Richard B. Russell Library for Political Research and Studies

sampled. Sampling can be done by appraisal or processing archivists. Normally, when processing manuscripts, archivists start with the largest unit and then work down to smaller divisions. But if bulk can be eliminated through sampling, that is a good place to start (see chapter 4 section on sampling).

Files that will not be refoldered and reboxed and to which preservation steps such as removing staples will not be applied can also be processed quickly (for example, academy files). Series that receive this level of arrangement and have no restrictions could be opened for research even when the rest of the collection is closed. These files will take little time of the processing archivists. The legislative series will probably require the most time,

Figure 3.3. Removal/Relocation Sheet

RICHARD B. RUSSELL LIBRARY FOR POLITICAL RESEARCH AND STUDIES
The University of Georgia Libraries

REMOVAL/RELOCATION SHEET

Description of Item:_____

_____

_____

_____

_____

_____

_____

_____

_____

_____

_____

_____

_____

Has Been Removed From:_____

_____

_____

By:_____

For the Purpose Of:_____

_____

_____

Will Be Temporarily Located: ____   Permanently Relocated: ____

At:_____

_____

Date:_____

Reprinted with permission of the Richard B. Russell Library for Political Research and Studies

Figure 3.4. Photograph Removal Sheet

RICHARD B. RUSSELL LIBRARY FOR POLITICAL RESEARCH AND STUDIES
The University of Georgia Libraries

PHOTOGRAPH REMOVAL SHEET

Number of Photographs:_____

Identify as to Size, Content and Whether B/W or Color:_____

_____

_____

_____

_____

_____

_____

_____

_____

_____

_____

_____

Related Manuscript Material Pulled Also? If so, Describe:_____

_____

_____

_____

Removed From:_____

_____

Relocated To:_____

_____

Purpose:_____

Date:_____

Initials:_____

Reprinted with permission of the Richard B. Russell Library for Political Research and Studies

Figure 3.5. Removal Sheet

USING REMOVAL SHEETS

Removal sheets are to be used when removing an item or group of closely related items permanently from its original location in a series or a collection. This does **not** include the removal of obvious misfiles, or the routine re-arrangement often necessary when processing a series or collection. The most frequent use of removal sheets will be for removing photographs from related manuscript material or the removal of oversize items.

Orange markers will still be used to mark photographs that have been removed for copying; they will be accompanied by a photocopy on acid-free paper of each photograph, and a call slip will be prepared for each photograph and filed under "Special Charges" until the photograph is refiled. A similar procedure is used for items on exhibit; a charge slip is filled out for each item *as fully as possible,* with the white copy being filed under "Special Charges," the pink copy in the item's original location, and the yellow copy placed in that exhibit's file.

The actual removal of the material, preparation and filing of the removal sheets should be done *after* the series/collection has been arranged. Until that time, items should be marked with a *blank* copy of the removal sheet standing upright in the folder at the location of each item. It may be necessary to clip the item to the removal sheet with a plastic clip—this should **not** be done with photographs, or when an item could be damaged by this procedure.

Two copies of the removal sheet should be prepared for each item or closely related group of items—an original and **an acid-free photocopy. The** original removal sheet (which is already on acid-free paper) is filed in the item's original location, and the photocopy is filed with the item in its new location. The descriptive section of the removal sheet **should be filled out as fully as possible** (except for photographs, where the caption is sufficient), so the item can be clearly identified. This also holds true for the "removed from" and the "moved to" sections of the sheet. *Always* **sign (first** initial, last name) and date the removal sheet.

When using the removal sheet with photographs, there is one additional step; the photograph should be photocopied **onto the back of the original removal sheet before it is filed in the item's original location**. The descriptive section of the sheet should include the size of the photograph and

Figure 3.5. Removal Sheet (continued)

Removal sheet instructions (continued)

whether it is in black and white or in color, **and they should be marked as being** removed for the reason "nature of item."

Oversize material should be marked as being removed for the reason "Size." In the case of oversize photographs, they should be photocopied onto the back of the original removal sheet using the reduction option on the photocopier. If the photograph is too large to do this, make a partial photocopy of the most (visually) important area of the photograph. For oversize items, the removal sheets should be numbered, and this number written *lightly* on the corresponding item(s); this number should be enclosed in square brackets.

A copy of the removal sheet is appended to these instructions.

---

since the majority of the files are usually kept and processed at the folder level.

Physical arranging also includes making decisions about the proper housing and physical maintenance of materials. The processing archivist should determine what items need to be removed to other locations. Oversize items are to be flattened and filed in oversize folders. Photographs are to be removed and filed in the "photographs" location or sleeved in mylar if they are to remain in the original location in the files. A similar decision must be made for slides and negatives, as well as oversize photographs. Audio and video tapes, phonograph records, films, and computer disks and tapes must be housed in appropriate locations and containers. When items are removed from files, separation sheets are needed to indicate to researchers and staff what has been removed and its location (see Figures 3.3, 3.4 and 3.5). The identification of items that require conservation begins during the appraisal process and should continue through all aspects of arrangement. Each repository must develop procedures for preservation and conservation of materials. Such procedures must be applied to congressional papers as well.

Suggested Procedural Guidelines for Arrangement

Most repositories do not have sufficient processing space to work with all boxes of a large congressional papers collection at one time. Therefore,

Figure 3.5. Removal Sheet (continued)

SPECIAL COLLECTIONS
REMOVAL SHEET

The following item(s) [For photographs, include size and whether black & white or color]

_____

_____

_____

_____

_____

_____

_____

_____

_____

Has/have been removed from _____

_____

And moved to _____

_____

For reasons of: __ Size   __ Nature of item   __ Other (_____

Name _____   Date _____

Reprinted with permission of the Strom Thurmond Institute, Clemson University Libraries

the archivist must determine a plan of action (or attack some would say). At the Louisiana and Lower Mississippi Valley Collections (LLMVC), archivists work with congressional papers on the series level first. When the office has a proper records management plan, archivists begin processing with the PERSONAL/POLITICAL/OFFICIAL series. From this series much can be learned about the interests and activities of the Member, which serves as a background for processing the LEGISLATIVE and CONSTITUENT SERVICES series.

Once the papers have been appraised and non-archival series removed (if they came to the repository), LLMVC student assistants do preliminary processing. Under the direction of the processing archivist, students check the chronology of the files to determine if any files are in the wrong year, identify folders that seem to be in the wrong series, flag oversize and other items that might need to be removed or photocopied, photocopy *Congressional Record* pages that contain statements by the Member and newsclippings about the Member, and remove rusted paper clips and staples on correspondence. Assistants also photocopy any letters containing signatures of Presidents, remove the letters, replace them with the photocopies, and give the originals to the processing archivist.

The LLMVC processing archivist determines whether series should be arranged at the item level or folder level, reviews the work of the student assistants, and makes decisions regarding preservation needs.

Congressional papers processing archivists at the Richard B. Russell Library for Political Research and Studies, University of Georgia and the Modern Political Collections Department of the South Caroliniana Library, University of South Carolina, recommend the following procedures for arrangement:

1. inventory the collection at the box level and make a list of visible series and subseries;

2. take notes on types of material, the function of the series and subseries, subjects, restrictions required, series which might be sampled or weeded, estimates of dates and volume, and physical condition of the materials;

3. make recommendation for an arrangement plan based on original order, if possible, or logical order;

4. after plan is approved, begin looking for misplaced folders or series in the wrong chronological order and consolidate series — note shifts in materials; and

5. keep notes about potential subject headings and index terms.[24]

Audiovisual materials need special housing and should be separated from the papers. To indicate to researchers that material has been removed from the original order, separation sheets are inserted in the file where materials are removed. (See Figure 3.3, Separation Sheet, Storm Thurmond Collection, Clemson University and Figure 3.4, Photograph Removal Form, Richard B. Russell Library for Political Research and Studies, University of Georgia.)

In the Louisiana and Lower Mississippi Valley Collections there are papers of 14 senators who were in office before 1948. Except for one, all senators' papers are included with groups of family papers and were not processed according to current standards. The first congressional papers processed in the LLMVC according to the instructions in this manual are those of Senator Russell B. Long (RBL). His papers set the standards LLMVC follows for all congressional papers.

Senator Long's papers bulk in the period 1948–1986. LLMVC processing staff did folder level processing for all permanent archival files from Long's office. They also

• refoldered and reboxed all files,

• photocopied items on poor quality paper,

• removed oversize papers, flattened and filed in appropriate size location with removal slips in original file,

• kept most printed research materials in legislative files,

• requested CMS tapes from the Senate computer office,

• item indexed photos and audio/video tapes,

• reformatted video tapes,

• had scrapbooks microfilmed at the Senate,

• kept a sample of artifacts (plaques, mementos, etc.)

• kept a large sample of invitations accepted even though calendars and appointments have that information

• made box inventories by folder label for each series

• made a microfilm of guide, box and folder inventories, and photo index for sale to researchers, and

• published a guide to the RBL collection.

The LLMVC also received the papers of J. Bennett Johnston (JBJ), Louisiana senator, 1973 to 1996. His files from 1973 to 1986 were compared with RBL's in order to eliminate as much duplication as possible. In JBJ and RBL, many of the files contained duplicate printed background materials from the same lobbying organizations. Therefore, JBJ's copies were eliminated but the accompanying memo files of JBJ's legislative assistant were kept. At the beginning of any series in which duplicate materials were eliminated, a note explaining that is in the JBJ preliminary guide. JBJ's files from 1987 to the end of 1996 will be handled in their entirety the way RBL's were. Only JBJ's 1973 to 1986 files have been processed because those years correspond to the years that RBL was still in office. John Breaux was elected a Louisiana senator in 1987. If Breaux's papers come to the LLMVC, materials in Breaux's files that duplicate material in JBJ's files 1987 to the end of 1996 will be discarded. House Members' files in the LLMVC are treated similarly. Because Senator Breaux has always had an excellent records management program in his office, the processing of his papers will take significantly less time than

Senator Long's did. Such an approach to arrangement of congressional papers reduces bulk and decreases the time needed to process them.

Describing

The purpose of description of congressional papers is to guide the researcher to the materials which she or he needs and to aid the archival staff in locating those items. Multiple page inventories created contain narrative analyses of the collection's components.

Inventories/guides can be in-house only, published in paper (such as the *Guide to the Russell Billiu Long Collection*), published in microform (such as the microfiche "Inventories of the Henry M. Jackson Papers"), or published in a combination of paper and microform (such as the *Guide to the Mike Gravel Papers, 1957–1980* which includes a box and folder listing on microfiche). In addition to these in-house or published inventories/guides, repositories may have additional finding aids and indexes to the congressional papers on paper and in computer databases. The Frank Church Papers are indexed in a database developed with Q&A software. The Church database also contains the folder inventory of the collection. The Sam Nunn Papers at Emory University are accessed through a relational database created with Paradox 3 software. At Louisiana State University, there are box and folder inventories for most of the series in the Russell B. Long Papers in-house printed out from databases created with dBase III software. At Carnegie Mellon University, the papers of Senator H. John Heinz III are being preserved and made accessible through the Heinz Electronic Library Interactive Online System (HELIOS). The system provides a full-text and image, searchable, hypertext linked database through the university library's online information system. Researchers can access the system through the Internet.[25] Certainly the sizes of current congressional papers collections are ideal for the application of computer databases.

The theories of archival description and their practical application are thoroughly discussed in Frederic M. Miller's *Arranging and Describing Archives and Manuscripts* (Chicago: Society of American Archivists, 1990). Congressional papers archivists must be familiar with and use Miller's manual in their work. (Description is covered in Miller chapters 8, 9 and 10.) In conjunction with Miller, congressional papers archivists need to follow the guidelines in Steven L. Hensen, *Archives, Personal Papers and Manuscripts: A Cataloging Manual for Archival Repositories, Historical Societies and Manuscript Libraries*, 2nd ed. (Chicago: Society of American Archivists, 1989).

Hensen's manual, APPM, helps archivists combine archival rules with the *Anglo-American Cataloguing Rules*, 2nd ed. in order to standardize archival description.[26]

Intellectual and physical arrangement is combined with description to complete the processing of congressional papers and to create finding aids. The "Processing Manual" of the Richard B. Russell Library for Political Research and Studies, The University of Georgia, indicates that the processing staff should think in terms of three levels of processing control. Each level has an overall goal, and denotes the physical and intellectual control that should be achieved at each level (see Figure 3.5). Miller states that descriptive elements which give information about the records [papers], the origins and context of the papers, the archival actions taken and the descriptive controls created, should be present in the descriptive tools (accession form, inventory, guides, repository data base, and the bibliographic network entry). Such descriptive elements could be: title, dates, origin, content, discussion of arrangement, volume, finding aids created, languages, relation to other papers, format, condition, restrictions, location, user access, biography, provenance, acquisition date, accessioning date, processing status, preservation actions taken, and repository control number.[27]

Description is defined by Bellardo and Bellardo as:

> 1. The process of analyzing, organizing, and recording information that serves to identify, manage, locate, and explain the holdings of archives and manuscript repositories and the contexts and records systems from which those holdings were selected. 2. The written representations or products of the above process.[28]

Congressional papers can be arranged and described following the same procedures the repository follows for other manuscript groups. After the archivist has arranged the series, notes taken during the arrangement will be used to write the description of the papers. One of the most important rules in preparing finding aids to all manuscript groups is to be succinct but accurate. Researchers need to know the way to locate information and they must rely on the descriptions provided by archivists. However, it is not the archivist's job to interpret the information in the files to the researcher.

Inventories

The inventory is the primary means of analyzing the collection and is defined as:

> 1. A basic archival finding aid whose unit of entry is usually the series. An inventory generally includes a brief administrative history [or biography

Figure 3.6. Processing Levels of Control

PROCESSING LEVELS OF CONTROL

LEVEL 1

Physical Control:

accession number:	o assigned when collection arrives.
arrangement:	o existing arrangement examined.
boxes:	o original containers usually retained; containers labeled with source, identification of contents if known and accession number.
folders:	o original folders retained.

Intellectual Control:

records:	o accession form completed including brief, descriptive content notes. o preliminary inventory prepared.
access by researchers:	o collection usually not open; special restrictions noted.

Goal:
New collection should be controlled at this level within five working days of receipt under normal circumstances.

LEVEL 2

Physical Control:

location:	o collection placed in permanent location when work at this level complete.
arrangement:	o arrangement into series; containers and folders arranged; individual items in folders not usually arranged.
boxes:	o reboxed; containers carry identifying and descriptive labels at end of work at this level.
folders:	o refolder; folders will have basic folder titles, as well as series, box and folder numbers. Box lists completed.
conservation:	o emergency measures undertaken; clips should be replaced, surface cleaning may be done, rubberbands discarded, photocopying and encapsulation can be completed. Notes made for future work.

or historical note] of the organization(s) [individual(s)] whose records are being described as well as descriptions of the records [papers]. Series descriptions give as a minimum such data as title, inclusive dates, quantity, arrangement, relationships to other series, and scope and content notes. Inventories may also contain appendices that provide such supplementary

Figure 3.6. Processing Levels of Control (continued)

Intellectual Control:

records:　　　　　　　　o processing record sheet indicates extent
　　　　　　　　　　　　　of processing at this level.

description:　　　　　o preliminary description prepared
　　　　　　　　　　　　　containing content, series description
　　　　　　　　　　　　　and box lists.

access by researchers:　o collection for which this level of work
　　　　　　　　　　　　　completed ordinarily open except for
　　　　　　　　　　　　　special restriction.

Goal:
　　　To have collections made available for research as quickly as
possible and where conservation is not a priority.

LEVEL 3

Physical Control:

arrangement:　　　　　o detailed item count, RBR identification
　　　　　　　　　　　　　seal stamped.

boxes:　　　　　　　　o remain in containers used at Level 2;
　　　　　　　　　　　　　detailed box labels, including folder
　　　　　　　　　　　　　count.

folders:　　　　　　　o if not refoldered at Level 2, refolder
　　　　　　　　　　　　　into acid-free folders at this level.

conservation:　　　　o preservation copying completed;
　　　　　　　　　　　　　duplicates removed; fasteners replaced;
　　　　　　　　　　　　　non-emergency repairs executed; papers
　　　　　　　　　　　　　cleaned if not done at Level 2.

Intellectual Control:

records:　　　　　　　　o processing record sheet indicates extent
　　　　　　　　　　　　　of arrangement and description at this
　　　　　　　　　　　　　level.

description:　　　　　o finding aid updated.

access by researchers:　o collection open except for special
　　　　　　　　　　　　　restrictions.

Goal:
　　　The collection has been completely processed and basic
conservation measures performed. Some processing time may also be
devoted to re-processing collections for which arrangement and/or
description are not adequate.

*Reprinted with permission of the Richard B. Russell Library for Political Research and
Studies*

information as container lists, folder lists, a glossary of abbreviations and
special terms, lists of files units on special subjects, indexes, and classification
plans/schemes.[29]

The inventory should contain the following elements which are access points for researchers: title, inclusive and bulk dates, quantity, arrangement, relationships to other collections, language, restrictions, geographic areas covered, and appropriate citation. Figure 3.6 shows how these elements appear on the second page of the inventory of Senator Russell B. Long's Papers. Description of series and subseries composes the inventory/guide. Also included in the inventory/guide are the scope and content note, biography/historical note, index terms, and box and folder listings.

Biographical Note

The biography can be in narrative or chronological form. It can also be extensive or simple. In the *Guide to the Russell B. Long Collection,* the biography was written by Senator Long's biographer and is ten pages long. The *Guide to the Mike Gravel Papers* contains a "Biographical Outline" which gives dated highlights of the Senator's life and career. *The Frank Church Papers: A Summary Guide* includes a brief two page narrative biography and an extensive "Frank Church Chronology." The microfiche inventories to the papers of Senator Henry M. Jackson give narrative biographies for each segment of the Senator's life and career.

Scope and Content Note

Each inventory or summary guide should contain a "scope and content note" defined by Bellardo and Bellardo as "a narrative statement summarizing information on the characteristics of the described materials, including function and use as well as the kinds and types of information contained therein."[30]

The scope and content note in the *Guide to the Russell Billiu Long Collection* reads:

> The Russell Billiu Long Collection is composed of two subgroups: The Long Family Papers Subgroup and the Russell Billiu Long Papers Subgroup.
>
> Correspondence among family members, newspaper clippings, photographs, speeches, financial documents, writings and memorabilia covering the period 1912-1986 document the lives and activities of Huey Pierce Long, Early Kemp Long, George Shannon Long, Palmer Reid Long, Rose Lolita Long McFarland, and Rose McConnell Long, as well as Russell B. Long. Most notably missing from the Long Family Papers Subgroup are files from Rose McConnell Long's tenure as a United State Senator (1936-1937) after her husband's death. Researchers should refer to related

manuscript groups for more extensive files on Huey Pierce Long (Mss Group # 2005) and Earl Kemp Long (Mss Group # 3126).

Documenting Russell B. Long's career as a United States Senator (1948-1986) are correspondence, research files, writings, schedules and trip files, subject files, legislative files, agencies' files, voting records, press releases, speeches, photographs, films, video tapes, scrapbooks, special issue files, social events files, and campaign materials. The Russell Billiu Long Papers Subgroup contains materials on RBL's pre-Senate life as well as the files of Senate office staff members.

NOTE ON ARRANGEMENT: In 1979 RBL's office filing system was changed to a central files system. Items that had previously been filed under separate subject headings: General Legislative Files, Department and Independent Agency Files, Project Files and some Special Issue Files after 1978 were centralized. All files were thereafter alphabetically interfiled for these areas under subject headings.

For each series, oversize materials have been removed from the regular files and separated to the oversize files. Such items are indicated by separation slips within files.[31]

The scope and content note from the *Guide to the Mike Gravel Papers* reads in part:

The Mike Gravel Papers, 1957-1980, consist mainly of the records of the years 1969-1980 when Gravel served in the United States Senate as junior senator from Alaska. The papers document and reflect the major areas of work, interest, and concern of both Gravel himself and his staff members...

In addition to manuscript materials, the collection contains photographs and slides, audio tapes, video tapes and films, memorabilia, an extensive file of chronologically arranged newspaper clippings, and scrapbooks of clippings from various periods of Gravel's career in the Senate. Also of note are the issued and draft press releases, speech texts, and constituent newsletters in the Press Release series. There are yearly calendars in the Trip and Daily Schedule files which record many of Gravel's appointments during his years in the Senate. The sponsorship and cosponsorship notebooks in the Legislative Files series record vital information about bills sponsored and cosponsored by Gravel. The Roll Call Votes series contains the voting record of individual Senators for the 91st–96th Congress as compiled by the Senate Democratic Policy Committee.[32]

Series Descriptions

Examples of series descriptions are shown in the section "Guidelines for Arrangement and Description." The series descriptions should reflect the intellectual arrangement of the congressional papers collection as shown by the example inventories on pages 55–62.

Box and Folder Inventories (Lists)

Box and folder inventories should be compiled as part of the inventory/guide. Because of the length of such listings for congressional papers, many repositories now use databases to compile the lists and publish them on microfiche. Such box and folder inventories may be available only in the repository, while some published guides include a copy of the microfiche. Other repositories may have no printed or microform lists but simply allow researchers to access the databases in-house. A box and folder list might look similar to the example from the Senator Russell B. Long papers inventory (see Figure 3.7). The entire inventory of the Long papers, including the box and folder listings, is available on microfilm. Chapter 4 on arrangement and description of series makes suggestions for preparation of box and folder listings.

Indexes

Creating indexes to the inventories/guides and to the collection can be a very complex project. With certain relational databases the box and folder headings become the index. Researchers can search by keywords and phrases, therefore a separate subject/name index is not necessary. Records prepared for entry into OCLC or RLIN, and for on-line databases which use the USMARC-AMC format have exact specifications on entering subject and name headings. Figure 3.8 shows the subject headings for the Russell B. Long Collection as they appear in the on-line catalog of the Louisiana State University Libraries, which is NOTIS software based. In Chapter 4 suggestions are made as to which series in congressional papers should or should not have separate indexes. In many congressional papers repositories only the inventory is indexed. In the Senator Henry M. Jackson Papers inventory

> an *Index* lists personal and corporate names and substantive terms and phrases as they appear throughout the inventory. Because of the multiplicity of series and subgroups and the repetition of files for each year, it is recommended that researchers searching for specific names or subjects use the index. Researchers should also be aware that the name index is not an exhaustive list of correspondents, but shows rather, those subjects and major correspondents which appear on folder headings.[33]

Whether the index is to the inventory, the entire collection or only to parts of the collection, terms used should be standardized and follow an authority list. Repositories should develop in-house authority lists based on

Figure 3.7. Box and Folder Inventory Page

Recrd Loc	Box	Series	Beg_date	End_date	Description
==== ==	===	=============================	========	========	===
513 26	502	U.S. SENATE: Senate Offcie Files	85/00/00	85/00/00	Central Files: Environment (Superfund--Wetlands)
514 26	503	U.S. SENATE: Senate Office Files	85/00/00	85/00/00	Central Files: Fed. Property (Contracts)--Foreign Trade (Ref. Dat
515 26	504	U.S. SENATE: Senate Office Files	85/00/00	85/00/00	Central Files: For. Trade (Ref. Data)--Grant Announce. (Statewide)
516 26	505	U.S. SENATE: Senate Office Files	85/00/00	85/00/00	Central Files: Health & Safety (Medicaid)--Labor (Training)
517 26	506	U.S. SENATE: Senate Office Files	85/00/00	85/00/00	Central Files: Labor (Training)--Park & Wildlife (National)
518 26	507	U.S. SENATE: Senate Office Files	85/00/00	85/00/00	Central Files: Parks & Wildlife (Nat'l)--Pub. Relations (Nut File)
519 26	508	U.S. SENATE: Senate Office Files	85/00/00	85/00/00	Central Files: Public Relations (Retirement)--Taxation (Corporate)
520 26	509	U.S. SENATE: Senate Office Files	85/00/00	85/00/00	Central Files: Taxation (Credits--Pension Annuities)
521 26	510	U.S. SENATE: Senate Office Files	85/00/00	85/00/00	Central Files: Taxation (Real Estate)--Transportation (Aviation)
522 26	511	U.S. SENATE: Senate Office Files	85/00/00	85/00/00	Central Files: Transportation (Aviation--Conrail)
523 26	512	U.S. SENATE: Senate Office Files	85/00/00	85/00/00	Central Files: Transportation (Conrail--Ref.)
524 26	513	U.S. SENATE: Senate Office Files	85/00/00	85/00/00	Central Files: Transportation (Conrail (Ref)--Mass Transit)
525 26	514	U.S. SENATE: Senate Office Files	85/00/00	85/00/00	Central Files: Transportation (Mass Transit--Railroads)
526 26	515	U.S. SENATE: Senate Office Files	85/00/00	85/00/00	Central Files: Transportation (Railroads--Waterways)
527 26	516	U.S. SENATE: Senate Office Files	86/00/00	86/00/00	Central Files: Administration (RBL Personal)--Agriculture
528 26	517	U.S. SENATE: Senate Office Files	86/00/00	86/00/00	Central Files: Agriculture (Rice)--Civil Rights
529 26	518	U.S. SENATE: Senate Office Files	86/00/00	86/00/00	Central Files: Commerce--Energy (Coal)
530 26	519	U.S. SENATE: Senate Office Files	86/00/00	86/00/00	Central Files: Energy (Conservation)--Envioronment)
531 26	520	U.S. SENATE: Senate Office Files	86/00/00	86/00/00	Central Files: Environment--Foreign Trade (Import Restrictions)
532 26	521	U.S. SENATE: Senate Office Files	86/00/00	86/00/00	Central Files: Foreign Trade (Ref. Data)--Health & Safety
533 26	522	U.S. SENATE: Senate Office Files	86/00/00	86/00/00	Central Files: Health & Safety--Indians
534 26	523	U.S. SENATE: Senate Office Files	86/00/00	86/00/00	Central Files: Indians--Private Enterprise
535 26	524	U.S. SENATE: Senate Office Files	86/00/00	86/00/00	Central Files: Private Enterprise--Taxation
536 26	525	U.S. SENATE: Senate Office Files	86/00/00	86/00/00	Central Files: Taxation (Credits--Savings Accounts)
537 26	526	U.S. SENATE: Senate Office Files	86/00/00	86/00/00	Central Files: Taxation (State Tax)--Transportation
538 26	527	U.S. SENATE: Senate Office Files	86/00/00	86/00/00	Central Files: Transportation (Coast Guard--Cure)
539 26	528	U.S. SENATE: Senate Office Files	86/00/00	86/00/00	Central Files: ransportation (Maritime--Railroads)
540 26	529	U.S. SENATE: Senate Office Files	86/00/00	86/00/00	Central Files: Transportation (Railroads--55 foot Channel)
541 26	530	U.S. SENATE: Senate Office Files			Corps. of Engr-Project Files:Algiers Lock & Canal--Army (Flooding;
542 26	531	U.S. SENATE: Senate Office Files			Corps. of Engr. Proj.: Army Engr. Proj.-Atchafalaya Basin
543 26	532	U.S. SENATE: Senate Office Files			Corps. of Engr. Proj.:Atchafalaya Basin & Ship Canal--Bush Bayou
544 26	533	U.S. SENATE: Senate Office Files			Corps. of Engr. Proj.: Caddo/Bossier Port--Contracts/Awards

Reprinted with permission of the Louisiana and Lower Mississippi Valley Collections, LSU Libraries

Figure 3.8. On-line Catalog Subject Headings

```
Search Request: A=LONG RUSSELL                           LSU Libraries
ARCHIVE - Record 3 of 9 Entries Found                      Long View
-----------------------------------------------------------------------
Collection name Papers

Subjects:          Petroleum law and legislation.
                   Petroleum in submerged lands.
                   Employee stock options.
                   Inland water transportation.
                   Taxation--Law and legislation.
                   Louisiana--Politics and government--1951-
                   Bills (legislative)
                   Scrapbooks.
                   Photoprints.
                   Legislators--United States.
Preferred Citation:
                   Russell Billiu Long Papers, Mss. 3700, Louisiana and Lower
                   Mississippi Valley Collections, LSU Libraries, Baton Rouge,
------------------------------------------------ + Page 3 of 4 -------------
STArt over         BRIef view                          <F8>  FORward page
HELp               INDex                               <F7>  BACk page
OTHer options      MARk                                <F6>  NEXt record
                                                       <F5>  PREvious record
NEXT COMMAND:
```

Reprinted with permission of the Louisiana and Lower Mississippi Valley Collections, LSU Libraries

the most recent edition of the *Library of Congress Subject Headings* (LCSH).[34] Thesauri which have been developed to aid in the building of authority files are: *Art and Architecture Thesaurus (AAT)* from the Getty Art History Information Program; *Genre Terms: A Thesaurus for Use in Rare Book and Special Collections Cataloging, Provenance Evidence: Thesaurus for Use in Rare Book and Special Collections Cataloging,* and *Relator Terms for Rare Book, Manuscript and Special Collections Cataloging,* all available from the American Library Association, Rare Books and Manuscripts Section; and the *Form Terms for Archives and Manuscript Control,* from the Research Libraries Group. Standardization of indexing vocabulary assists researchers who do work in multiple repositories and the archival community. It also makes it possible to enter headings into OCLC or RLIN using the USMARC-AMC format.[35]

USMARC-AMC

The USMARC Format for Archival and Manuscripts Control is:

a USM-ARC format, endorsed by the Society of American Archivists, for the exchange of descriptive and administrative information about archival materials. The format popularly known as the AMC Format, is jointly administered by the Society of American Archivists and the Library of Congress. The USMARC Format is: a communications format developed

Figure 3.9. USMARC-AMC On-line Catalog Record

```
LTMD MORE                                                    AFL5590
                              NOTIS CATALOGING                    L544
MD- AFL5590 FMT U RT b BL c DT 02/21/95 R/DT none    STAT mc E/L   DCF a D/S C
SRC d PLACE lau LANG eng MOD    REPRO    D/CODE i DT/1 1912 DT/2 1990

035/1:   :  |9 (MD)AEV4200
040:     :  |a LU |c LU |e appm
090/1:   :  |a Mss. 3700
100:1 :  |a Long, Russell B.
245:10:  |a Papers, |f 1912-1990.
300/1:   :  |a 771 |f linear ft.
351/1:   :  |a Subgroups and series: I. Long Family Papers (1912-1986, n.d.): 1.
Huey Pierce Long Papers (1912-1985); 2. Earl Kemp Long Papers (1939-1962); Long
Family Papers (1935-1986); II. Russell Billiu Long Papers (1912-1990): 1. Early
Years (1920-1948); 2. Executive Counsel to Earl Kemp Long Papers (1947-1948);
3. U.S. Senate (1948-1990); 4. Political (1947-1988); 5. Social (1949-1986)
545/1:   :  |a U.S. Senator and lawyer from Shreveport, Louisiana.
520/2:   :  |a Correspondence, legislative files, committee files, federal
agency files, special project files, political campaign files, press releases,
speeches, audio tapes, motion picture film, videotapes, photographs, and other
materials.


    LTMD MORE                                                AFL5590
                                  NOTIS CATALOGING                L544

    520/3:   :  |a The papers relate chiefly to Long's Senate career and the work of
his Senate office staff on national issues and Louisiana affairs.  Also
included are several thousand items relating to the personal and political
activities of the Long family, particularly Huey Long, Russell's father.
    520/4:   :  |a Major topics include tax reform, petroleum and legislation,
patents and government-developed inventions, petroleum in submerged lands,
flood control, inland water transportation, Louisiana politics and government,
and employee stock options.
    540/5:   :  |a Physical rights are retained by the LSU Libraries. Copyright is
retained in accordance with U.S. copyright laws.
    555/6:0 :  |a Available in the library.
    524:    :  |a Russell Billiu Long Papers, Mss. 3700, Louisiana and Lower
Mississippi Valley Collections, LSU Libraries, Baton Rouge, La.
    650/1: 0:  |a Petroleum law and legislation.
    650/2: 0:  |a Petroleum in submerged lands.
    651/3: 0:  |a Louisiana |x Politics and government |y 1951-
    650/4: 0:  |a Employee stock options.
    600/5:10:  |a Long, Huey Pierce, |d 1893-1935.
    650/6: 0:  |a Inland water transportation.


    LTMD DONE                                                AFL5590
                                  NOTIS CATALOGING                L544

    655/7: 7:  |a Bills (legislative) |2 ftamc
    655/8: 7:  |a Scrapbooks. |2 ftamc
    655/9: 7:  |a Photoprints. |2 ftamc
    650/10: 0:  |a Taxation |x Law and legislation.
    656/11: 7:  |a Legislators |z United States. |2 lcsh
    851/1:   :  |a Louisiana and Lower Mississippi Valley Collections, |a LSU
Libraries, Baton Rouge, LA 70803-3300
```

Reprinted with permission of the Louisiana and Lower Mississippi Valley Collections, LSU Libraries

at the Library of Congress for producing and distributing machine-readable bibliographic records on magnetic tape.[36]

The bibliographic utilities OCLC and RLIN use USMARC Formats for entering records on materials within libraries. In order to use OCLC or RLIN and most library on-line databases, archivists must follow the USMARC-AMC format. Figure 3.9 shows the USMARC Archival and

Figure 3.10. On-line Catalog Record Researcher View

```
Search Request: A=LONG RUSSELL                              LSU Libraries
ARCHIVE - Record 3 of 9 Entries Found                       Long View
---------------------------------------------------------------------------
Creator:          Long, Russell B.
Collection Name:
                  Papers, 1912-1990.
Description:       771 linear ft.
Organization:     Subgroups and series: I. Long Family Papers (1912-1986, n.d.):
                  1. Huey Pierce Long Papers (1912-1985); 2. Earl Kemp Long
                  Papers (1939-1962); Long Family Papers (1935-1986); II.
                  Russell Billiu Long Papers (1912-1990): 1. Early Years
                  (1920-1948); 2. Executive Counsel to Earl Kemp Long Papers
                  (1947-1948); 3. U.S. Senate (1948-1990); 4. Political (1947-
                  1988); 5. Social (1949-1986)
Biographical/Historical Note:
                  U.S. Senator and lawyer from Shreveport, Louisiana.
Summary:          Correspondence, legislative files, committee files, federal
                  agency files, special project files, political campaign
------------------------------------------------ + Page 1 of 4 -------------
STArt over          BRIef view                        <F8>  FORward page
HELp                INDex                              <F6>  NEXt record
OTHer options       MARk                               <F5>  PREvious record

NEXT COMMAND:


Search Request: A=LONG RUSSELL                              LSU Libraries
ARCHIVE - Record 3 of 9 Entries Found                       Long View
---------------------------------------------------------------------------
Collection name Papers

Summary:          files, press releases, speeches, audio tapes, motion picture
                  film, videotapes, photographs, and other materials.
                  The papers relate chiefly to Long's Senate career and the work
                  of his Senate office staff on national issues and Louisiana
                  affairs.  Also included are several thousand items relating
                  to the personal and political activities of the Long family,
                  particularly Huey Long, Russell's father.
                  Major topics include tax reform, petroleum law and
                  legislation, patents and government-developed inventions,
                  petroleum in submerged lands, flood control, inland water
                  transportation, Louisiana politics and government, and
                  employee stock options.
Subjects:         Long, Huey Pierce, 1893-1935.
------------------------------------------------ + Page 2 of 4 -------------
STArt over          BRIef view                        <F8>  FORward page
HELp                INDex                              <F7>  BACk page
OTHer options       MARk                               <F6>  NEXt record
                                                       <F5>  PREvious record
NEXT COMMAND:
```

Reprinted with permission of the Louisiana and Lower Mississippi Valley Collections, LSU Libraries

Manuscripts Control Format record for the Senator Russell B. Long Collection at Louisiana State University. The LSU Libraries use an on-line catalog which operates with NOTIS software. Figure 3.10 shows how the Russell B. Long record looks to a researcher using the LSU on-line library catalog.

When the USMARC-AMC format records are to be added to the OCLC or RLIN national database by the repository, these records must follow the appropriate standards. The American Heritage Center, University of Wyoming, has published an extremely helpful manual for OCLC cataloging.[37]

In addition to these national databases, manuscript repositories should send information about their collections of congressional papers to the *National Union Catalog of Manuscript Collections* (NUCMC) maintained by the Library of Congress. NUCMC entries were formerly published in bound volumes (1959 to 1990) but currently are available only through RLIN. Repositories, however, do not have to be members of RLIN to report their collections to NUCMC. NUCMC will provide repositories with forms to complete from which NUCMC staff enter the records.[38]

Databases

Some of the database software that has been used by congressional repositories are Q&A, Paradox and dBase. All have similar properties and each repository should evaluate the software to be used based on its individual needs.

In the Special Collections Department of the Emory University Libraries, Paradox 3 is the database used for developing the relational database for the papers of Senator Sam Nunn. Congressional Archivist Naomi L. Nelson states that the relational database is critical for managing the archival records of Senator Nunn, who is still in office:

> I have been working with the Nunn Papers to develop a system that will both meet the Senator's immediate needs and be readily applicable to our other Congressional collections. As Senator Nunn is still in office, he requires quick access to the records we hold. In addition, our procedures must accommodate continual additions to open series, as his office sends us several shipments of records per year. Our main challenges are as follows: speed and accuracy of retrieval, linking records of different formats that document the same event (e.g., transcripts, photographs, background materials and audio recording of a particular speech), linking records that concern the same issue or subject matter (e.g., all records regarding gun control), and allowing for differing levels of description for different series. To address these challenges, we have developed an intellectual organizational scheme and a computer database. For the intellectual organization, we used the types of "Files of Permanent Historical Value" listed in Karen Paul's *Records Management Handbook for United States Senators and Their Repositories* as series headings, maintaining the broad division of the file types into 5 categories (which we use as subgroup headings). We renamed "Administrative Files" to "Constituent Services" and added subgroups for "Pre-Congressional" and "Subject Files." Our finding aids consist of a guide, box list, folder list, and inventory in linked relational databases. The user can move from a Guide entry to the related box list or folder list by pressing a button. In the inventory, the user can move from an entry to

Figure 3.11. Sam Nunn Congressional Database

SAM NUNN CONGRESSIONAL COLLECTION DATABASE

Copyright c 1992 by Emory University
Designed by Naomi L. Nelson

This database was constructed on Paradox 3.5 in order to provide faster and more precise access to the records in the Sam Nunn Congressional Collection. Initial system requirements included:

o   ability to tailor the level of description to the needs of individual series or subseries. (For example, constituent correspondence is described to the level of the box list, while the Subject Files are given folder level descriptions and assigned subject and geographic location headings.)

o   integration of the shelf list with the other finding aids so that changes in arrangement are entered only once.

o   searching mechanism allowing Special Collections staff to search for particular items without knowing how to use Paradox.

o   multi-level password protection permitting read-only privileges for some users and editing privileges for others.

o   ability to generate box labels, cassette labels, and other types of labels so that information entered in the system can be used to label the collection quickly and accurately

o   ability to generate hard-copy indexes to the database's contents

o   system compatibility with the database software used in Senator Nunn's DC office allowing the exchange of information

---

the subjects, geographic locations, or federal agencies associated with that entry.[39]

Figures 3.11 and 3.12 give information about the Sam Nunn Congressional Collection Database.[40] Although a thorough records management plan is in place in the office and only archival records are forwarded to the library, many times Senator Nunn's office needs to refer to files in the archives. Because this can happen with the papers of any sitting senator or representative, finding aids need to be accessible to office staff as well as to repository archivists and researchers.

All such descriptive activities enable the congressional papers archivist

Figure 3.11. Sam Nunn Congressional Database (continued)

SAM NUNN CONGRESSIONAL COLLECTION
SPECIAL COLLECTIONS, WOODRUFF LIBRARY, EMORY UNIVERSITY

System *access points* include:

o   Subject (based on the Legislative Indexing Vocabulary)

o   Geographic location

o   Federal departments, agencies, or commissions involved (D/A)

o   Span dates

o   Broad topic (based on the topics used in SN's office)

o   Key word in title or description

The database consists of two related, but separate, sets of tables. The first set comprises a *guide*, *boxlist*, and *itemlist* for the series in the Nunn Congressional Collection. The user can toggle between these three tables and can query them separately or in tandem. The second set of tables comprises an *inventory* of selected series within in the Nunn Collection. The inventory provides access through subject, geographic location and federal department or commission involved. Eventually, the two sets of tables will be linked so that the user can move seamlessly from one to the other.

Reprinted with permission of Special Collections, Woodruff Library, Emory University

to maintain intellectual and physical control over the collections and to make these materials available to researchers as needed.

NOTES

1. Paul, *The Documentation of Congress*, 2–3.
2. *Ibid.*, 14.
3. Aronsson, "Appraisal," 81.
4. Bellardo and Bellardo, *A Glossary*, 1.
5. "Processing Manual," Richard B. Russell Library for Political Research and Studies, The University of Georgia, 1994, 2–4.

Figure 3.12. Relationship Between the Nunn Finding Aids Sam Nunn Congressional Database

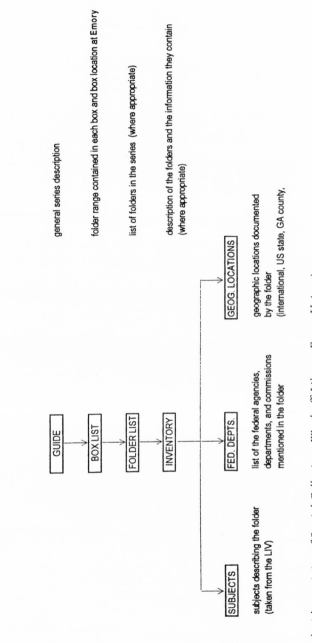

RELATIONSHIP BETWEEN THE NUNN COLLECTION FINDING AIDS

GUIDE — general series description

BOX LIST — folder range contained in each box and box location at Emory

FOLDER LIST — list of folders in the series (where appropriate)

INVENTORY — description of the folders and the information they contain (where appropriate)

FED. DEPTS. — list of the federal agencies, departments, and commissions mentioned in the folder

GEOG. LOCATIONS — geographic locations documented by the folder (international, US state, GA county,

SUBJECTS — subjects describing the folder (taken from the LIV)

6. Fredric M. Miller, *Arranging and Describing Archives and Manuscripts* (Chicago: Society of American Archivists, 1990), 31.

7. *Ibid.*, 39–40.

8. *Ibid.*, 3–10, 31–44.

9. *Ibid.*

10. *Ibid.*

11. *Ibid.*, 7.

12. Bellardo and Bellardo, *A Glossary*, 4.

13. Oliver W. Holmes, "Archival Arrangement — Five Different Operations at Five Different Levels," *American Archivist* 27 (January 1964): 21–41.

14. Miller, *Arranging and Describing*, 58–60.

15. Paul, *The Documentation of Congress*, 22.

16. Bellardo and Bellardo, *A Glossary*, 32.

17. *Ibid.*, 34.

18. Miller, *Arranging and Describing*, 62–63.

19. *Ibid.*, 68.

20. Gallagher, "A Repository Archivist," 49–58.

21. The American Heritage Center at the University of Wyoming has an excellent "Processing Manual" which is not just for congressional papers but for all their collections. The Richard B. Russell Library for Political Research and Studies also has an excellent "Processing Manual" specifically for congressional papers.

22. See for example, Frank Boles, "Disrespecting Original Order," *American Archivist* 45 (Winter 1982): 26–32.

23. Ralph W. Hansen and Deborah J. Roberts, *The Frank Church Papers* (Boise, Idaho: Boise State University Library, 1988), 8.

24. "Processing Manual," Richard B. Russell Library for Political Research and Studies, University of Georgia, 3; and "Processing Guidelines," Modern Political Collections, South Caroliniana Library, University of South Carolina, 2–3.

25. Edward Galloway, "News from Carnegie Mellon University — The Heinz Archives," *Society of American Archivists Congressional Papers Roundtable Newsletter* (November 1994): 4–5.

26. Michael Gorman and Paul W. Winkler, eds., *Anglo-American Cataloguing Rules*, 2nd edition, revised (Chicago: American Library Association, 1988).

27. Miller, *Arranging and Describing*, 83–89.

28. Bellardo and Bellardo, *A Glossary*, 10.

29. *Ibid.*, 19.

30. *Ibid.*, 31.

31. Phillips and Ford, *Russell B. Long Collection Guide.*

32. Barbara M. Tabbert, *Guide to the Mike Gravel Papers, 1957–1980* (Fairbanks, AK: University of Alaska–Fairbanks, Elmer E. Rasmuson Library, 1986), 3–4.

33. "Henry M. Jackson Papers Inventories" (Seattle: University of Washington Libraries, 1989), 2.

34. Library of Congress, Subject Cataloging Division, *Library of Congress Subject Headings*, 10th ed. (Washington: Library of Congress, 1986).

35. The *Art and Architecture Thesaurus* (New York: Oxford University Press, 1990) is available in 3 volumes or on disk. AAT includes the RLG *Form Terms for Archival and Manuscript Control* as well as a list of terms describing activities, processes and functions of records and record creators in state archives collections.

36. Bellardo and Bellardo, *A Glossary*, 36.

37. Maxine Trost, *Archives and Manuscripts OCLC Cataloging Manual* (Laramie, WY: American Heritage Center, 1991).

38. Write to NUCMC, Library of Congress, Washington, D.C. 20540.

39. Naomi L. Nelson to the author, April 14, 1994. In the same letter Nelson states that "The Senator's office files from 1972–1978 were arranged in one central file according to the *Files Handbook for Congressional Offices, Senate Members* published by the National Archives and Records Service's Office of Records Management (1968). These files include records belonging to several of the subgroups defined in the *Records Management Handbook* and, rather than trying to divide this series up, we decided to create a special subgroup containing all the subject files with cross-references to other subgroups."

40. Naomi L. Nelson, creator, "Sam Nunn Congressional Collection Database Description," Special Collections, Robert W. Woodruff Library, Emory University, revised October 1993.

CHAPTER 4

Guidelines for Arrangement and Description

This section discusses the series found in congressional papers and the arrangement, description, and preservation of the types of documents within the series. These series and their arrangement within groups and subgroups, as well as possible arrangements for subseries, are shown in the model inventories, Chapter 3, pages 55–62.

The format for this section is as follows:

Example: Example of a series description from a finding aid [inventory] for congressional papers [for example from the Senator Russell B. Long Papers inventory]. These examples will include the series description as written and will identify the series location in the group's arrangement by subgroup [Legislative, etc.], series [Legislative Assistants' Files, etc.], subseries, and subsubseries.

Other locations: lists other series where the same type of files might be found or other series where the same file might be duplicated.

Types of documents included: lists the various documents which could be included in the series.

Arrangement: gives suggestions for the physical and intellectual arrangement of the series.

Preservation: gives suggestions for the improvement of the physical condition of the series.[1]

Description: gives suggestions for information to include in the finding aids for the series.

The examples are intended to be just that — examples. Congressional papers archivists should follow the arrangement of files that was used in the office. If the original order is lost or if the office has poor or no records

91

management the examples might be used for possible guidelines in arranging and describing the files.

Examples for this section are taken from:

The Frank Church Papers: A Summary Guide, Special Collections Department, Boise State University Library, 1988;

Guide to the Mike Gravel Papers, 1957–1980, Alaska and Polar Regions Department, Elmer E. Rasmuson Library, University of Alaska–Fairbanks, 1986;

"Inventory, Olin Dewitt Talmadge Johnston Papers, 1923–1965," Modern Political Collections, South Caroliniana Library, University of South Carolina, 1991;

"Inventories, Henry M. Jackson Papers," Manuscripts and University Archives, University of Washington Libraries, 1990; *Russell Billiu Long Collection Guide*," Louisiana and Lower Mississippi Valley Collections, Louisiana State University, 1995; and

"The Sam B. Hall, Jr. Papers," 1990, and "The Jack Hightower Papers," 1989, rev. 1990, Political Collections Library, Baylor University.

A full citation is given only for the first entry from each guide.

Notes on the Senator Russell B. Long Collection

Some of the examples given in this section are from the Senator Russell B. Long Collection in the Louisiana and Lower Mississippi Valley Collections of the Louisiana State University Libraries. Physical arrangement of boxes on a shelf is not sacrosanct. The inventory/guide is an intellectual arrangement on paper to show relationships of one series/subseries to another. This intellectual arrangement is also to aid the researcher. Where items sit in relationship to one another on a shelf does not dictate intellectual arrangement of the inventory/guide. Nor should physical arrangement dictate intellectual description — they really are separate issues. Most often in today's repositories, large collections will not physically be housed on the shelf in exactly the same order that the intellectual arrangement appears in the inventory/guide. Boxes in the same series may be several shelves or floors or even buildings apart and internal management systems tell the reference staff where to go to physically retrieve a particular box. In-house box inventories may even inform the researchers as to which shelf a box sits on, but the interpretation of that information is for repository staff only. Except for making it possible for the staff to bring the person the correct box, physical location is intellectually irrelevant to the researchers. Senator Long's papers are actually physically arranged on the shelves the way they are intellectually described in the guide. But box lists are separate from the guide and available as a separate microfilm publication or in-house access aid. Long's will be the last large collection that LLMVC will be able to arrange physically on the shelves to match completely the intellectual arrangement of the guide.

The examples in this section show the arrangement and description of the files from Long's senate office. The arrangement reflects the original order of the files as they were received from that office. The only changes to the original order at the series and file levels has been to correct obvious misfiles. There were, of course, some files with no labels or visible series connection. This will be true of almost any set of congressional papers. These "unidentified" files were reviewed by the processing archivist to determine proper location or to determine if they could be discarded. In some cases such "unidentified" files will need to be incorporated into a miscellany file.

The first records management handbook for senators appeared in 1985. Before that senators had received assistance from the Senate Historical Office, the Library of Congress, some contract archivists, and repositories regarding the arrangement and records management of their files, but there was really no model. Therefore, most senators' office files were (see the example from the introduction to the Frank Church Papers, p. 63), and maybe still are, the reflections of staff organizations and individual files management. In some cases, such as in the office of Senator Long, an extremely efficient and strong office manager developed and controlled the records management and files management within the office. She followed Senate records management guidelines and hired a professional contract archivist to assist with the transfer of records to the repository at Louisiana State University. However, she did establish a "Central Files" system in 1979 which was in two sections. One section was for issue/constituent mail. These were the letters routinely answered by CMS and original constituent letters were discarded at the end of each calendar year. The second section contained what the staff had formerly filed in several other categories (such as "General Legislative" and "Department and Independent Agencies").

Personal/Political/Official Papers[2]

Aronsson states that the title "personal office files" is really a misnomer, for members of Congress rarely keep files of a truly personal nature. Such files are labeled "personal" because they contain the material brought to the attention of the member.[3] While the senator or representative may not actually "create" the files, they come to exist because of the interests and activities of the "person." Included are appointments and schedules, diaries or other writings, files of the personal and appointment secretary, the member's VIP and family correspondence, telephone logs and memos, biographical materials as well as clippings and scrapbooks, invitations, and subject files of special interest to the member.

Also included in the personal office files may be campaign committee files, party and political leadership files, and VIP appointment files. Files associated with campaigning and political parties detail the member's involvement in establishing "a leadership and an internal organization that facilitates priority setting, policy formulation, and consensus building."[4] Some offices may categorize staff or personnel files and other things such as routine vouchers as part of the personal office files. Intellectual description of such office administration files is clearer when separate from personal files.

> The senator's or representative's personal files are valuable for the insights they provide about the member's activities while an elected official. The personal files reflect the senator's or representative's lifestyle and ways of interacting with cohorts, and they contribute to a researcher's understanding of the senator or representative as a person.[5]

Personal/Political/Official

APPOINTMENT BOOKS, DAILY SCHEDULES, DESK CALENDARS:
appraised as permanent

EXAMPLE: Senator Russell B. Long Collection, Louisiana State University[6]
Russell Billiu Long Collection [group]
    Russell B. Long Papers, 1912–1990 (bulk dates 1948–1986) (658 lf) [sub group]
        United States Senate, 1948–1990 (bulk dates 1949–1986) (618.5 lf) [series]
            Senate Office Files, 1948–1989 (bulk dates 1949–1986) (608 lf) [sub-series]
                Personal Office Files, 1948–1991 (34 lf) [sub-subseries]
                    Schedules and Calendars, 1956–1986 (5 lf) [sub-sub-sub-series]
Includes daily schedules, monthly schedules of meetings, trips schedules, daily logs and yearly calendars for RBL.

EXAMPLE: Senator Mike Gravel Papers, University of Alaska–Fairbanks[7]
Mike Gravel Papers [group]
  Office Records [sub-group]
    Trip and Daily Schedule Files, 1969–1980 [series]
      Appointment Calendars and Guest Books [subseries]
Consists of six boxes of various styles of appointment calendars kept by Gravel and his staff over the years that he was in office. There are calendars for every year of Gravel's Senate tenure except 1980. For some years there are several calendars, some of which are far more detailed than others. From the handwriting, it appears that the more detailed calendars were kept by the Senator's personal secretary and the sketchy ones by the Senator himself. They should be consulted in connection with the daily schedule files and the trip files for a complete record of his schedule. In addition to the appointment calendars, this subseries also includes six guest books of a miscellaneous nature: some are identified as to event and date and others are totally without identification. The Appointment Calendar Books and Guest Books subseries is arranged in roughly chronological order.

Other locations: Other daily agendas, appointments, and schedules can be found in Russell Long's PERSONAL SECRETARIES' FILES. In other collections they might be located in ADMINISTRATIVE ASSISTANTS' FILES, APPOINTMENT SECRETARIES' FILES, TRIP FILES and/or PRESS FILES.

Types of documents included: This series could include a record of daily appointments in notebook form, computer diskettes, or desk calendars with annotations.

Arrangement: The most common arrangement is chronological. These files need minimum arrangement except to determine what years are included.

Preservation: These will come in all sizes, shapes, and formats. If possible box together, but folder only if needed to maintain loose pages. If post-it notes are included on pages, photocopy the information and place the copy in the calendar where the post-it note was located. Remove clips if possible, but retain notes where they are found. When the calendar is in computer format (tape or diskette), handle according to electronic records procedures. These should be indicated "archival" on the computer as they are created.

Description: The title of this subseries identifies it thoroughly. Include dates and any unusual facts about the materials (e.g., cartoons drawn by the assistants; etc.). Also cross reference to other subseries when appropriate, as with Russell Long, whose Personal Secretary also kept separate calendars and appointment books.

> PERSONAL DIARIES, JOURNALS: appraised as permanent
> WRITINGS AND MANUSCRIPTS: appraised as permanent

EXAMPLE: Senator Frank Church Papers, Boise State University[8]
Frank Church Papers [group]
    Speeches, Articles, Trips and Meetings, 1941-1980 (41 boxes) [series]
        Articles and Magazines (4 boxes) [sub-series]
This file contains articles written by Senator Church, some of which were based upon speeches he had given that were expanded for publication. The article files are indexed in three ways: alphabetically by the title of the article, the name of the publication in which they appeared, and by date. The controversial January 26, 1965, *Look* article, "Conspiracy USA," can be found in this portion of the collection.

EXAMPLE: Senator Russell B. Long Collection, Louisiana State University
Russell B. Long Papers [subgroup]
    United States Senate [series]
        Senate Office Files [subseries]
            Personal Office Files [sub-subseries]
                Writings, 1978–1982, n.d. (1 lf) [RESTRICTED] [sub-sub-subseries]
Because of the sensitive nature of many items, this series is restricted until 2010. The series consists of notes mostly handwritten by RBL. Some appear to be drafts of personal letters, while others appear to be notes for speeches. A few photocopies are included but most items are originals. A few of the items are addressed "Dear Mr. P" and discuss such issues as welfare reform, economics, and the energy crisis. These may have been intended for the President of the United States or the President of the United States Senate. Other draft letters are addressed to family members giving advice and discussing RBL's beliefs in marriage and religion. Some discuss HPL's and RBL's decisions to enter politics.

Russell Long kept no diary or journal while in the Senate. He did, however, write notes to himself and write letters like those described above. The Senator does not recall who some of the letters were intended for and knows that some were never sent. Many of these items were found in the Senator's that some were never sent. Many of these items were found in the Senator's desk when the office closed. Most were kept by his personal secretary when she found them and were originally labeled "Notes — RBL."

Other locations: Can be found in PERSONAL SECRETARIES' FILES, CAMPAIGN FILES, FAMILY PAPERS, or ADMINISTRATIVE ASSISTANTS' FILES.

Types of documents included: This series could include diaries or personal journals, manuscript diaries, dictation, or transcripts of dictation, notes, articles for publication and drafts of those articles, and books written by the member.

Arrangement: The arrangement for PERSONAL DIARIES most accurate is chronological. JOURNALS may be arranged according to topic or chronology. Both may be on audio tape recorded by the member or in electronic format with paper transcripts and printouts. Arrange the paper copies chronologically or topically as the original order shows. If electronic, the PERSONAL DIARIES and JOURNALS should have been indicated as "archival" on the computer as they were created. WRITINGS AND MANUSCRIPTS will be more difficult to arrange. If dated, arrange them chronologically. If topics are assigned to the material, arrange them topically or by subject. WRITINGS for publication can be arranged by title alphabetically. In the Russell Long papers, the WRITINGS are arranged by type, such as notes, draft letters, etc., and then chronologically when possible.

Preservation: Because of the variety of formats of materials found in these files, preservation and housing will need to be viewed from that standpoint. If the DIARIES/JOURNALS/WRITINGS are on audio tapes, follow the guidelines for storage of audio tapes. If they are electronic, follow the guidelines for electronic records. Paper files should be handled routinely but watch for enclosures such as post-it notes and newspapers clippings. Photocopy these as necessary. Because of the personal insight these give about a senator or representative, they should receive careful physical attention. Remove clips and staples and flatten any folded items. House volumes in appropriate sized boxes.

Description: Again, because these DIARIES/JOURNALS/WRITINGS provide insight into the personality of the Member, they should receive a thorough description. For routine DIARIES in a chronological arrangement, give a description of the kind of information contained in the diary: notes by senator on legislation, notes by representative on activities of friends and family, analysis of the day's events, etc. For unusual types of materials such as those in the Russell Long files, give an explanation of what is contained and why. For WRITINGS AND MANUSCRIPTS, which are copies of articles or books for publication, the title will be sufficient description.

PERSONAL SECRETARIES' FILES: usually appraised as staff files which are permanent, with careful weeding.

EXAMPLE: Senator Russell B. Long Collection, Louisiana State University
   Personal Office Files [sub-subseries]
   Personal Secretaries' Files, 1949–1986 (2.5 lf) [sub-sub-subseries]

Includes correspondence to and from constituents and agency personnel to RBL's personal secretaries; memos to RBL and notes from RBL; general files include copies of speeches and drafts of speeches (1966–1970), press releases, daily agendas, appointments and schedules; and telephone messages. Also includes file heading lists and mail analysis for 1976–1986 and a list of former staff members, 1945–1986.

Other locations: Such files may be found or duplicated in STAFF FILES, MEMBER'S CORRESPONDENCE, VIP CORRESPONDENCE, CENTRAL FILES, SUBJECT/TOPICAL FILES, CHRONOLOGICAL FILES, TRIP FILES, ADMINISTRATIVE ASSISTANTS' FILES, or MISCELLANEOUS FILES.

Arrangement: Depending on the types of files in the PERSONAL SECRETARIES' FILES, these will most often be chronologically or subject arranged. Use file headings as found and original order when possible. Memos to and notes from the member and any VIP correspondence should be arranged at the item level. Other files in this series do not need to be arranged at the item level.

Preservation: For memos to and notes from the member, photocopy items on "bad" paper, and VIP correspondence. "Bad" paper is newsprint, onion skin, colored paper, cardboard, or mimeo paper. Separate photographs. One of RBL's secretaries had the most unarchival and annoying habit of taking small pieces of paper with telephone messages or appointment notes to herself or to the senator and stapling them onto 8×11 three ring binder paper and then placing these in a three ring binder filed chronologically. Many times there were notes written by the secretary on the sheet where the note was stapled. These notes are very insightful into the daily activities of the senator and the decision was made to retain all the pages. Because of the staples, tape and poor condition of the note papers, the decision was made to photocopy all pages, of which there were only several hundred. A sample of the original pages has been retained for clarification of the type of file that existed.

Description: Briefly state what is included, list subjects of file folder head-

CORRESPONDENCE — VIP — MEMBERS': appraised as permanent

EXAMPLE: Senator Russell B. Long Collection, Louisiana State University
  Personal Office Files [sub-subseries]
    Correspondence, 1948–1987 (9 lf) [sub-sub-subseries]
    Included are some constituent mail, correspondence from colleagues on
various political issues, and personal mail from colleagues. The letters are
filed alphabetically by last name of the author and then chronologically by
year. VIP letters pertain to legislative issues and RBL's view concerning issues.
VIP letters have been photocopied and originals placed in the vault. This
series includes Christmas cards and thank-you letters. Includes some post-
Senate materials.

EXAMPLE: Senator Mike Gravel Papers, University of Alaska–Fairbanks
  Mike Gravel Papers [group]
    Correspondence [subgroup]
      General Correspondence [series]
        Letters from Well-known Persons, 1974–1980, and Interoffice
        Memorandums, 1974-1975 and 1979-1980 [subseries]
    Contains two unrelated folders. The first folder contains letters to Sen-
ator Gravel from prominent people, mostly politicians, such as Presidents
Ford and Carter and other Senators. However, there are some letters from
people in other walks of life, such as Norman Mailer and Jack Valenti. The
second folder contains interoffice memorandums which were written by various staff members in 1974-75 and 1979-80. There is no indication that similar staff memorandums were kept separately during the other years of
Gravel's tenure in office.

Other locations: Such files may also be found in the PERSONAL SEC-
RETARIES' FILES, STAFF FILES, ADMINISTRATIVE ASSISTANTS'
FILES, or CENTRAL FILES.
  Types of documents included: Correspondence with family members, colleagues, and personal friends and associates, memos and telephone notes and
messages. May contain correspondence and telephone messages from VIPs;
federal, state, and local officials; community leaders; etc., pertaining to legislative issues and the member's views concerning issues and his or her efforts
on behalf of VIP constituents.[9] Might also include name lists of VIPs and
photograph directory or index.
  Arrangement: Alphabetical by name and then chronological. These
files should be arranged at the item level when they contain original

files should be arranged at the item level when they contain original correspondence from VIPs. Remove unidentified photographs. Separate oversize items.

Preservation: Photocopy VIP letters and separate originals which may be in danger of theft because of their autograph value. Photocopy clippings. Separate photographs to be retained or enclose in mylar.

Description: This series would benefit from a name index in the guide or as an addendum to the inventory. Describe contents, note any unique files or any unusual gaps in the files. Note arrangement and if any indexes exist for the series.

TELEPHONE—MEMOS OF CONVERSATIONS, LOGS: appraised as permanent

EXAMPLE: Senator Russell B. Long Collection, Louisiana State University
Personal Office Files [sub-subseries]
Telephone Logs, 1959–1981 (2 lf) [sub-sub-subseries]
Each staff member kept a "Weekly Report to Senator Long" which lists the name of the party telephoning, who they represented, what topic was discussed, date, time and staff members' names. RBL and administrative staff reviewed these to stay informed with constituents' concerns.

Other locations: Such telephone logs or memos may appear in the PERSONAL SECRETARIES' FILES, ADMINISTRATIVE ASSISTANTS' FILES, CORRESPONDENCE — VIPs — MEMBERS', or STAFF FILES.

Types of documents included: May include telephone report sheets, memos for the file detailing conversations, and logs.

Arrangement: Filed by topic, name of individual, or by date. If these files contain significant amounts of information, arrangement may need to take place at the item level. In most cases, however, such materials should be arranged only at the folder level.

Preservation: Loose leaf pages should be handled routinely. If the logs are in a book format that cannot be separated, house in appropriate sized boxes.

Description: Give an overview of how extensive the information contained in the files is, e.g., name and phone number only included, caller's opinion regarding legislation noted, etc.

BIOGRAPHICAL FILES: appraised as permanent with weeding for dupli-

EXAMPLE: Senator Frank Church Papers, Boise State University
  Frank Church Papers [group]
    Personal (30 boxes) [series]
      Biographical, 1956–1987 (1 box) [subseries]
      Biographical material has been sorted into two units. The first unit contains material produced by the Church office or the Church campaign committees. The second section is comprised of published stories from newspapers and magazines.

Other locations: Can also be located in PRESS FILES, PERSONAL SECRETARIES' FILES, ADMINISTRATIVE ASSISTANTS' FILES, STAFF FILES, SCRAPBOOKS, or CLIPPINGS.

Types of documents included: biographical sheets, life histories, resumes, articles and newspaper clippings.

Arrangement: Arrange most documents chronologically, and remove duplicates. If articles and newspaper clippings are included, an alphabetical file by name of publication can be used. Item level arrangement is not necessary.

Preservation: Photocopy clippings and magazine articles on poor quality paper, remove photographs or place in mylar folders.

Description: For researchers these files will be a starting point in research about a particular member of Congress. Explain what types of documents are included, cross reference to other locations for biographical materials.

SCRAPBOOKS: appraised as permanent with microfilming recommended

EXAMPLE: Senator Russell B. Long Collection, Louisiana State University
  Press, 1948–1990 (bulk dates 1949–1986) (92.5 lf) [sub-subseries]
    Scrapbooks, 1947–1983 (l lf) [sub-sub-subseries]
    In addition to clippings, a series of scrapbooks were kept by the Senator's office for a number of years. Due to their poor condition, all the scrapbooks were microfilmed by the Senate Microfilming Department. Newspaper clippings about RBL, and clippings and magazine articles about RBL's family are included. Two scrapbooks were retained.

EXAMPLE: Senator Frank Church Papers, Boise State University
  Frank Church Papers [group]
    Public Relations (64 boxes and 42 volumes) [series]
      Newspaper Clippings and Scrapbooks [subseries]
        Scrapbooks (42 volumes) [sub-subseries]

January 1957–May 1976. (Lacking 1/62–5/62, 4/70–6/70, and 5/73–7/73.) General clippings, in chronological order, of events in which Senator Church's name appeared in the story. Five volumes are topical and concern 1) Vietnam, 2) Church's 1960 keynote address, 3) Steve Symms and 4) Church's presidential campaign in 1976 (2 vols.).

Other locations: Might also be found in PERSONAL SECRETARIES' FILES, PRESS or PUBLIC RELATIONS.

Types of documents included: Items that highlight the member's career such as newsclippings (most frequently), letters from VIPs, photographs, some invitations, magazine articles, and sometimes memorabilia.

Arrangement: Scrapbooks should be maintained as they are received unless they have been taken apart or have fallen apart. Then arrange chronologically as with clippings.

Preservation: Microfilm. Paul states that "Senators' scrapbooks are best preserved if archival quality scrapbooks, are used initially. Older scrapbooks should be reproduced, to preserve the information and to limit the handling of the scrapbooks, by microfilming onto 35mm film (using a planetary camera) or by photocopying onto archival quality bond paper."[10]

Description: For scrapbooks, give only a brief overview of what they contain and why they were created. If the scrapbooks are subject scrapbooks dealing with certain activities, describe the activity and the reason why the scrapbook was created. Cross reference subject scrapbooks.

PARTY LEADERSHIP FILES: appraised as permanent

EXAMPLE: Senator Russell B. Long Collection, Louisiana State University
   United States Senate [series]
      Senate Assistant Majority Leader Files, 1964–1971 (.05 lf) [subseries]
   In 1964, RBL was elected by his colleagues to serve as Senate Assistant Majority Leader (Senate Whip). Files include correspondence of support for RBL, correspondence from RBL soliciting support from other Senators, congratulatory letters, and agendas. One group of correspondence from RBL denies the 1968 rumor that he had resigned as Assistant Majority Leader.

      Senate Committee Files, 1957–1986 (11 lf) [subseries]
         Democratic Steering Committee Files, 1968–1982 (3 inches) [sub-
         subseries]
      The Senate Democratic Steering Committee was responsible for making appointments of Senators to various committees. These files include

correspondence regarding committee preference, lists of possible members, and final committee assignments.

EXAMPLE: United States Representative Jack Hightower Papers, Baylor University[11]

Jack Hightower Papers [group]
  1974–1984, Congressional Files [subgroup]
    House of Representatives Organization Files, 1974–1984 (3.75 lf)
    [series]
Correspondence, printed material, and newsclippings from 1974–1984 concerning the administration of the House of Representatives and activities of the Democratic leadership, various caucuses, study groups, and other organizations which Hightower participated in. Much of the general correspondence concerns elections to leadership positions and selections to committees.

Other locations: Copies of these files may be located in other files but most often they should be filed separately within the PERSONAL OFFICE FILES.

Types of documents included: Correspondence, memos, briefing materials, position papers, whip notices, daily schedules, committee assignment files, head counts, member lists, agendas, joint leadership session information and other materials relating to the leadership.

Arrangement: Maintain original order if possible. Weed at the item level for duplicates. Most will be chronologically by Congress and then alphabetically by name of correspondent or by subject.

Preservation: Photocopy clippings, etc. Separate photographs or sleeve in mylar.

Description: Include subjects. Name indexes are probably not necessary because this type of material is usually circulated to all party members in the senate or house. The exception may be to note VIPs other than members corresponded with. In the above example from RBL, the completed guide describes the Democratic Steering Committee Files as a sub-subseries under the subseries Senate Committee Files. This is a descriptive error for these are party leadership files. A cross reference in the in-house inventory under committee files and Senate Assistant Majority Leader Files will hopefully alleviate any confusion for the researchers.

CAUCUS/POLITICAL PARTY RECORDS: appraised as permanent with careful weeding recommended

EXAMPLE: Senator Russell B. Long Collection, Louisiana State University
Political Series, 1947–1988 (18.5 lf) [series]
Democratic National Party and National Campaign Files, 1956–1980
(4.5 lf) [subseries]
Includes Democratic and Republican platforms, background informa-
tion, speeches, articles, convention files, voting records of candidates for
President, and correspondence.

EXAMPLE: Senator Frank Church, Boise State University
Frank Church Papers [group]
Political Affairs (13 boxes) [series]
Political affairs are primarily files on party politics on both the local and
national level, including material on the various elections and delegate selection for the various Democratic National Conventions. Most are dated 1957-
1969, with some exceptions such as Watergate, which dates from 1973-1974.
Also included are files on prominent Idaho Democrats and Church's political opponents. The Political Affairs series complements the Issue Books in
the Public Relations series, the Special Files in the Personal series and the
Campaign series.

EXAMPLE: Senator Mike Gravel Papers, University of Alaska–Fairbanks
Senator Mike Gravel Papers [group]
Campaign [subgroup]
Democratic National Convention, 1972 (6 document boxes, 3 lf)
Alphabetically arranged [series]
Convention Delegates [sub-series]
Convention: General [sub-series]
The Democratic National Convention series details Gravel's 1972 bid
for the Vice-Presidential nomination. Subseries 1 contains lists of delegates
from all states to the 1972 Democratic Convention in Miami. Included with
these lists are many handwritten notes concerning contacts Gravel's staff
made with many of these delegates and notes of staff perceptions as to
whether the contacted delegate would or would not support Gravel in his
bid for the nomination. Arrangement in this subseries is alphabetical by the
names of the states that the listed delegates represented. Subseries 2 includes
a conventions schedule, miscellaneous clippings, a copy of Gravel's speech
to the convention, correspondence, and staff memorandums. The subseries
is arranged alphabetically by subject.

Other locations: May be found in ADMINISTRATIVE ASSISTANTS'

FILES, CAMPAIGN FILES, PUBLIC RELATIONS, PRESS FILES, STAFF FILES, PARTY LEADERSHIP FILES, CAMPAIGN FILES or PERSONAL SECRETARIES' FILES.

Types of documents included: Correspondence, memos, notes, lists, convention schedules, clippings, copies of speeches, study papers, transcripts of minutes of meetings, research materials, publicity files, financial records, campaign training materials, and briefing materials pertaining to party or caucus matters, legislative service organizations or party policy organizations.

Arrangement: Arrange alphabetically by name of organization or group, then alphabetically by name of correspondent or subject within the organization or group. Remove duplicates but do not arrange at item level. Remove unidentified photographs.

Preservation: Photocopy clippings and poor quality paper in caucus files. Do not photocopy routine clippings in national party files. Sleeve identified photographs in Mylar or remove to photograph files.

Description: Be sure to identify organizations and groups represented. Some explanation as to function of the group may be needed. Cross reference to other such files.

CAMPAIGN FILES: appraised as permanent with careful weeding

EXAMPLE: Senator Russell B. Long Collection, Louisiana State University
   Political Series, 1947–1988 (18.5 lf) [series]
   Senate Campaign Files, 1948–1981 (9 lf) [subseries]
   Includes correspondence to and from constituents, newsletters, clippings, speeches, biographical information, interview transcripts, transcripts of commercial, and tabular reports on Louisiana voters.

EXAMPLE: Senator Frank Church Papers, Boise State University
   Frank Church Papers [group]
      Campaigns (32 boxes) [series]
         1956–74 Senatorial Elections [subseries]
         1976 Presidential Nomination Campaign [subseries]
         1980 Senatorial Election [subseries]
         1968–1980 Polls [subseries]
   This series contains campaign files of Senator Church and his staff. It includes material on advertising, volunteers, fund raising and donors, issues, clippings, speech material and speeches, files on opponents, polls, press

releases and financial disclosures. See also Campaign Manager Carl Burke's collection and the Audio Visual material for campaign media.

The Frank Church Audio-Visual Collection [series]
    The Video Collection [subseries]
        Campaigns [sub-subseries]
    This series contains mostly 30-second and one minute campaign advertisements. There are a few longer *Face the Nation, Meet the Press* and comparable Idaho programs. Many such appearances were only recorded on audio tape and can be found in the Audio Collection.

The Audio Collection [subseries]
    Campaigns [sub-series]
    The campaign recordings contain sound tracks for campaign commercials, news interviews and speeches both by Church and his supporters and Church's opponents and critics.

EXAMPLE: Senator Mike Gravel Papers, University of Alaska–Fairbanks
    Mike Gravel Papers [group]
        Campaign [subgroup]
            Friends of Mike Gravel, 1967–1980 (63 document boxes, 26 lf)
            Arrangement varies. [series]
                1967–1969 [subseries 1]
                — — — —
                1980 [subseries 10]
    The Friends of Mike Gravel series contains financial records and related materials documenting the activity of six separate fundraising and campaign committees that existed at various times during Gravel's Senate tenure. These committees are: The Alaskan Committee, Alaskans for Gravel, Alaskans for the Reelection of Mike Gravel, Friends of Mike Gravel–Senate, Friends of Mike Gravel–Vice President, Supporters of Mike Gravel. Each one of the subseries listed above, which are chronologically arranged, is divided into some or all of the following categories, which are arranged in alphabetical order: accounting, advertising, campaign, contributors, correspondence, election, expenses, fundraisers, issues and receipts.

Other locations: CAMPAIGN FILES may unfortunately be filed in many separate places such as the PRESS SECRETARIES' FILES, PRESS FILES, ADMINISTRATIVE ASSISTANTS' FILES, PERSONAL SECRETARIES' FILES, or even MISCELLANEOUS. One Louisiana senator's press secretary traveled with him throughout campaigns and many campaign committee files wound up interspersed through PRESS FILES.

Types of documents included: Correspondence, memos, clipping files, position and strategy papers, election returns, polling data, schedules and calendars, photographs, audio and video tapes of interviews and political advertisements, campaign contributions data and spending reports, public opinion surveys, direct mailings, and related items.

Arrangement: Maintain original order if possible. If not, arrange chronologically by campaign year, then alphabetically by subject. Arrange photographs and audiovisual materials by type of record. These files can probably be reduced by careful weeding for duplicates.

Preservation: For paper, preservation is routine. The nonpaper records in these files cause the same problems they cause in the PRESS FILES. See Karen Paul, *Records Management Handbook*, Chapter V, for information on preservation of special media.

Description: List campaign years represented and then subjects. Cross-reference any CAMPAIGN FILES appearing in other files.

INVITATIONS: appraised in various ways, most often that accepted invitations for senators be permanent. (Many repositories have made the decision to discard these or to sample them. See Chapter 5 for information on sampling.)

EXAMPLE: Senator Russell B. Long Collection, Louisiana State University
    Personal Office Files [sub-subseries]
        Invitations Accepted, 1948–1986 (4 lf) [sub-sub-subseries]
        Over his 38 years in office, Senator Long accepted numerous invitations to official and nonofficial functions. His attendance at these functions is reflected in his schedules and calendars, therefore the invitations files were randomly sampled for each year. The retained invitations are arranged chronologically. Nonaccepted invitations were disposed of in Washington according to the office records management plan.

EXAMPLE: Senator Mike Gravel Papers, University of Alaska–Fairbanks
    Mike Gravel Papers [group]
        Office Records [subgroup]
            Trip and Daily Schedules, 1969–1980 (56 document boxes, 23 lf)
            Arrangement varies. [series]
                Daily Schedule Files [subseries]
            The Trip and Daily Schedule series contains the detailed daily records

of how Senator Gravel spent his time while he was a member of the Senate. The Daily Schedule Files subseries contains a separate folder for each month of the year that Gravel was in office. The folders are arranged chronologically. Each contains detailed daily schedules prepared by Gravel's office listing appointments and obligations for any given day. Also in these folders are a sampling of the invitations that Gravel received to all kinds of events.

Other locations: INVITATIONS FILES can also be found in PRESS FILES, TRIP FILES, PERSONAL SECRETARIES' FILES, COMMITTEE FILES, CAMPAIGN FILES, PARTY LEADERSHIP FILES, CORRESPONDENCE FILES or ADMINISTRATIVE ASSISTANTS' FILES.

Types of documents included: Requests for appearances at an event or for a meeting with the senator (other than official Senate activities such as presiding over the Senate and attending committee meetings).[12] May include correspondence, cards, posters, brochures, summary or registers of accepted and declined invitations, schedules, agendas and itineraries.

Arrangement: Follow sampling guidelines or retain all accepted invitations. Can be arranged chronologically or alphabetically by name of individual or organization. Remove and photocopy any VIP signed original invitations — especially presidential. Follow original order if possible. Do not arrange at the item level. Senator Long's office sent to the repository over 19 linear feet of invitations in chronological order by year. RBL's schedules, calendars and trip files fully reflect invitations he did accept and some that he did not accept but to which he sent staff members in his place. Therefore, the repository made a decision to sample the accepted invitations (see section on sampling).

Preservation: With RBL the decision was made not to do any preservation work such as photocopying of poor quality papers. The office had filed them and taken good care of the files but the invitations were all sizes from 3x5 card size to legal size paper, printed on heavy card stock with colored inks and everything in between, down all the way to colored construction papers. This decision is open to reassessment of the retained files at a later date.

Description: Briefly describe what is included and if sampled. Cross reference to schedule and trip files. Do not create name indexes or item inventories.

According to Aronsson:

> Invitations require special attention by the archivist because some (those that were accepted) merit preservation while others (those that were rejected) do not. Accepted invitations reveal the activities of an individual

member of Congress and also may help a researcher identify categories of social events attended by high-level federal officials. Many archivists and historians argue that rejected invitations are of value, too, because they identify those organizations that a member of Congress did not think were of sufficient importance to warrant his support. Most representatives and senators cannot possibly accept all of the invitations they receive, and their reasons for turning down any given invitation would be almost impossible to determine. Researchers who want to study rejected invitations can identify these invitations by going through the computerized indexes of the office's correspondence.[13]

JOB RECOMMENDATIONS/APPOINTMENTS FILES: VIP appointments, judgeships, and other high level government appointments appraised as permanent subject to access restrictions

EXAMPLE: Senator Russell B. Long Collection, Louisiana State University
  Personal Office Files [sub-subseries]
    Miscellaneous Files, 1966–1982 (5 lf) [sub-sub-subseries]
      Judgeship Files, 1949–1987 (2 lf) [sub-sub-sub-subseries]
    Letters of nomination written by RBL for Federal judgeships; requests for letters of recommendation; and background files.

EXAMPLE: Senator Mike Gravel Papers, University of Alaska–Fairbanks
  Mike Gravel Papers [group]
    Constituent Services [subgroup]
      Requests for Federal Appointments, 1977 (3 document boxes, 1 lf)
        Alphabetically arranged. Restricted. [series]
    After the election of President Jimmy Carter in 1976, Senator Gravel's office received a large number of requests for federal appointments, primarily from Alaskan Democrats, but also some from individuals in other states. This series contains supporting resumés and, frequently, letters of recommendation. There is very little information in the series about appointments which were actually made. Boxes 760 and 761 contain general requests from Alaskans seeking appointments. Box 762 contains more specific requests for particular positions from Alaskans and non-Alaskans as well as Gravel's endorsements of some candidates. Arrangement of the series is alphabetical by folder title. The folder contents are roughly alphabetical, but no attempt was made to ensure that exact alphabetical order exists. Because of the personal nature of the materials, this series is restricted.

Other locations: RECOMMENDATIONS/APPOINTMENT FILES

may also be found in CORRESPONDENCE FILES and PERSONAL SEC-
RETARY'S FILES.

Arrangement: Weed all but those related to VIP or former staff appointments and judgeships. Arrange alphabetically by name.

Preservation: Photocopy items on poor quality paper, remove clips and
staples. If photographs are included that are to be retained, sleeve in Mylar.
Photocopy clippings.

Description: While a separate index of the names included would be
helpful for research, these files do not warrant such intensive description. Be
sure to note access restrictions relating to privacy of individuals.

TRIP FILES: appraised as permanent with weeding recommended

EXAMPLE: Senator Frank Church Papers, Boise State University
  Frank Church Papers [group}
    Speeches, Articles, Trips and Meetings, 1941–1980 [series]
      Trip Files (20 boxes) [subseries]
    Chronological files of Senatorial, personal and vacation trips taken by
the Senator and his family. Trips are identified by the destination and sponsor.

EXAMPLE: Senator Mike Gravel Papers, University of Alaska–Fairbanks
  Mike Gravel Papers [group}
    Office Records [subgroup]
    Trip and Daily Schedules, 1969–1980 (56 document boxes, 23 lf) [series]
      Trip Files [subseries]
    Gravel traveled a great deal during his tenure in the Senate, and the
Senator's trip files document the arrangements for his trips, contacts made,
and business accomplished while traveling. These files have not been extensively processed and they remain in the original order in which they were
kept by Gravel's staff. Gravel's trip files generally contain detailed schedules
for trips, often background information about the places to be visited, people to be seen, and conferences to be attended. There are sometimes invitations, lists of people to be thanked, fundraising contacts, and copies of
thank-you letters that were eventually sent. The trip files are chronologically arranged, and each folder is labeled with the date of the trip and the
destination.

EXAMPLE: United States Representative Sam B. Hall, Jr., Baylor University[14]
  Sam B. Hall, Jr., Papers [group]

Trips, 1977–1984 (2.5 lf) [series]

Files on trips consist of 2.5 linear feet of correspondence, printed material, and newsclippings concerning preparations, itineraries, activities, and news coverage. Hall's trips documented here were mostly in association with activities of the Judiciary Committee, the Veterans Affairs Committee, and the Select committee on Narcotics Abuse and Control.

Other locations: These files may be combined with APPOINTMENTS, SCHEDULES, or PRESS FILES and in CAMPAIGN FILES.

Types of documents included: May include correspondence, schedules, itineraries, agendas, invitations, lists, financial records, and research materials.

Arrangement: Maintain original order but weed for duplicate materials. Arrange chronologically at the folder level. These files should be reviewed at a later date for further weeding or discarding.

Preservation: Since many of the items in these files will be duplicated or summarized elsewhere, retain in original folders and do no preservation work. If photographs are to be retained in the series, however, sleeve in Mylar.

Description: Give a general and brief overview of what is contained and cross reference to files that summarize trips such as schedule files.

FINANCIAL DISCLOSURE REPORTS: appraised as permanent

EXAMPLE: Senator Frank Church Papers, Boise State University
   Frank Church Papers [group]
      Personal (30 boxes) [subgroup]
         Financial Disclosure (one box) [series]

Senator Church supported financial disclosure for public officials and he voluntarily disclosed his finances before such a course was mandated by federal law. The Collection contains disclosure information for 1961–1980. Further financial disclosure records can be found in the Campaign files.

Other locations: CAMPAIGN FILES, PERSONAL SECRETARIES' FILES, and OFFICE MANAGERS' FILES.

Types of documents included: These are annual financial disclosure report forms filed according to Senate and House rules relating to the provisions of Title I of the Ethics in Government Act of 1978.

Arrangement: File chronologically, remove duplicates.

Preservation: Photocopy items on poor quality paper, remove paper clips and staples.

Description: State that they are report forms filed according to Senate and House rules. List years represented.

MISCELLANEOUS/SUBJECT/TOPICAL FILES: different appraisals, most are permanent with weeding recommended

EXAMPLE: Senator Russell B. Long Collection, Louisiana State University
Senate Office Files [subseries]
    Personal Office Files [sub-subseries]
        Miscellaneous Files, 1966–1982 (5 lf) [sub-sub-subseries]
            Tom Dodd Controversy Files, 1966–1967 (2 lf) [sub-sub-sub-subseries]

In 1967, Senator Thomas J. Dodd of Connecticut was investigated by the Senate Select Committee on Standards and Conduct. RBL was a proponent of Dodd's innocence. Files include legal briefs, bills and resolutions, research material, press releases, speeches, memos, newsletters, drafts of newsletters and correspondence.

Social Series, 1949–1986 (14.5 lf)
    Mardi Gras Files, 1955–1986 (9 lf) [subseries]
Each year the Louisiana delegation hosted a Mardi Gras celebration in Washington, D.C. RBL's office handled the arrangements. Included are correspondence, lists of attendees and members of the Krewe of Louisianans, programs, financial records, reservations, and information on arrangement. RBL's actual Mardi Gras costume is included in this series.

Other Social Occasions Files, 1963–1984 (1.5 lf) [subseries]
    Louisiana State Society Picnic Files, 1963–1969 (6 inches) [sub-subseries]
These yearly picnics held in Washington, D.C., were fund raising events for RBL. Included are invitations, lists of attendees, and correspondence.

New Orleans World's Fair, 1974–1984 (1 lf) [sub-subseries]
In 1984, a World's Fair was held in New Orleans after ten years of planning. These files include planning documents, economic studies, correspondence with constituents and company representatives, calendars of events, and publications of the Fair.

Memorabilia, 1949–1986 (6 lf) [subseries]
During his career RBL was presented with hundreds of plaques,

certificates, citations, and other items from organizations he spoke to and from political supporters. A representative sample of these items was kept.

EXAMPLE: Senator Frank Church Papers, Boise State University
Frank Church Papers [group]
   Personal (30 boxes) [series]
      Special Files (8 boxes) [subseries]
      Files containing background material on then-current legislation, topics for which Church had committee assignments or topics which he wished to be informed about. Some of this material was in expanding files, making them easy to extract for a committee meeting or ready reference. Dates on the files are for limited chronological periods, further suggesting their immediate utility. See also Issue Books.

EXAMPLE: Senator Mike Gravel Papers, University of Alaska–Fairbanks
Mike Gravel Papers [group]
   Public Relations [subgroup]
      Miscellaneous Memorabilia, 1969–1980 (2 flat boxes, 1 lf)
      Unarranged. [series]
      This series contains a variety of objects, primarily desk items, such as paperweights and pen sets, that were given to Senator Gravel at various times during his political career. There is also a small box of miscellaneous campaign buttons from both Gravel's campaigns for the Senate and from other Alaskan political campaigns. There is also a pencil drawing of Senator Gravel by an artist who signed the drawing "Hutch." Many of the items are not personalized, but some do specifically name Gravel. The items are together in one large box, except for the campaign buttons, which are boxed separately. A complete listing of the items in the series appears in the container list for the collection.

A number of examples are given for this series because it can represent so many different categories from legislation to personal interests. As the processing guidelines for the Modern Political Collections at the South Caroliniana Library state:

> Miscellaneous is that hodgepodge of material which doesn't appear to have great historical merit and doesn't fit easily into a standard series; don't worry if this catchall category seems too large. As you work through a collection you will be able to place much of this material into appropriate series, and discard a good bit of the remainder, but you will always have a batch of material you feel should be retained, but have no logical place other than miscellany for it.[15]

In the RBL collection, archivists chose to put the Tom Dodd Controversy Files in the MISCELLANEOUS FILES under the United States Senate Series, PERSONAL OFFICE FILES subseries, because they dealt directly with a Senate issue. In the RBL MISCELLANEOUS FILES of the PERSONAL OFFICE FILES, they also placed JUDGESHIP FILES and SERVICE ACADEMY FILES. These last two sets of files could have been described as subseries under PERSONAL OFFICE FILES and not under a MISCELLANEOUS FILES category. The Social Series in RBL could all have been described under MISCELLANEOUS FILES. The Louisiana State Society Picnic Files could have been described under CAMPAIGN FILES instead of in this separate series. Had the picnic files been the only social events files in RBL, the archivists would have probably intellectually arranged and described them under CAMPAIGN FILES.

Other locations: Special interest, topical or subject files, miscellany and memorabilia can be found in PRESS FILES, CAMPAIGN FILES, PERSONAL SECRETARIES' FILES, PUBLIC RELATIONS FILES, TRIP FILES, and INVITATIONS.

Types of documents included: Almost any type of document could appear in this series: legislative documents and background research, correspondence, invitations, notes and writings, photographs and clippings, and three-dimensional objects.

Arrangement: For subject and topical paper files, arrange by subject at the folder level. Do not arrange at the item level. Remove duplicates and separate bulky items such as campaign buttons. Sample artifacts such as plaques and awards.

Preservation: Paper should be handled routinely. Artifacts should be evaluated carefully before being retained. Photocopy certificates. If photographs are to be retained with files, sleeve in Mylar. Photocopy clippings if not numerous.

Description: Subject files and topical files should be described thoroughly as to contents and cross referenced to other appropriate files. Artifacts should receive only a brief description and should not be listed.

NON-CONGRESSIONAL PERSONAL FILES—appraisal is dependent on the contents.

Although these files should be located in a separate subgroup from congressional papers, some repositories have chosen to include them with congressional papers.

EXAMPLE: United States Representative Jack Hightower Papers, Baylor University
  Jack Hightower Papers [group]
    1974–1984, Congressional Files [subgroup]
      Personal Files, 1974–1984 (26.25 lf) [series]

Included in this series are files which either deal with Hightower's non-Congressional activities, such as the Baylor University Board of Trustees files; were designated as personal correspondence; or reflect formal recognitions and honors. They consist of correspondence, speeches, and financial records, 1974–1984.

The arrangement, preservation and description of noncongressional personal files that are included with congressional papers should be based on the repositories' standard procedures for other manuscript collections. Of course, many of the suggestions contained in this manual for the arrangement and description of congressional papers can apply to noncongressional papers as well.

Legislative Files

The United States House of Representatives' "Guidelines for the Disposition of Members' Papers" states that "Legislative files are the heart of the collection. Those and files closely pertaining to them should receive the highest consideration. They reflect what the Member was elected to do and the issues which were important to the nation and the district and state at that time."[16] Certainly appraisal guidelines emphasize that legislative files are to be preserved almost in their entirety because of their research value.

The authors of *The Documentation of Congress* explain each congressional function:

> The legislative function encompasses all of the legislative responsibilities set forth in the Constitution together with those that have evolved more recently. This function includes the formulation and passage of bills that become law, including revenue bills and appropriations measures; the "executive" function of providing advice and consent on nominations and treaties; the "judicial" function of impeachment; the oversight function; the investigative function; and the budgetary function.[17]

LEGISLATIVE SUBJECT (TOPICAL) FILES AND BACKGROUND RESEARCH: appraised as permanent with some weeding necessary

EXAMPLE: Senator Russell B. Long Collection, Louisiana State University
Russell B. Long Collection [group]
   Russell B. Long Papers [subgroup]
      United States Senate Series [series]
         Senate Office Files [subseries]
            Legislative Files, 1949–1986 (151 lf) [sub-subseries]
               General Legislative Files, 1949–1978 (137 lf) [sub-sub-sub-
               series]

These files contain correspondence from constituents expressing their opinions about various bills and amendments and RBL's response to them; letters and notes from colleagues in the House and Senate seeking support, or thanking RBL for support for certain bills, resolutions and amendments; letters and telegrams from lobbyists, agencies, organizations, and businesses; copies of research and background information from constituents, colleagues, agencies, organizations, businesses, and lobbyists; copies of bills, amendments, resolutions and pages of the *Congressional Record*; includes some handwritten notes from RBL and staff members. These files are arranged chronologically by year and then alphabetically within years. See guide to General Legislative Files by subject, available in repository. [After 1978 the office developed a system of Central Files. General Legislative Files for 1979-1986 will be found in the Central Files.]

EXAMPLE: Senator Frank Church Papers, Boise State University
Frank Church Papers [group]
   Legislation Files, 1956–80 (162 boxes and 20 notebooks) [subgroup]

Senator Church's legislative files are arranged alphabetically by subject. Many issues will be found in more than one place in the Legislation files, depending on the aspect being treated or the volume of correspondence or the whim of the filing staff that day. As a result, the computerized subject index to the collection will be essential for exhaustive retrieval of information. For example, the Basques appear in the Legislation files as sheepherders with immigration problems and as wool raisers who want protection from foreign wool. Because of the Basques' longstanding ties to Spain, a significant amount of material is found in the Foreign Relations Committee files, and immigration problems surface in the Immigration and Naturalization Service files of the Federal Government series. In the same way, the issues of, for instance, natural resources, forests and forestry, timber and lumber are so interrelated that information about wood can be found under each heading.

EXAMPLE: Senator Olin D. T. Johnston Papers, University of South Carolina
Olin D. T. Johnston Papers [group]
Legislative Files, 121.25 lf [series]
Contain correspondence and other material relating to bills and issues considered by Congress. Files often include copies of the pertinent bills and resolutions, committee prints, and official and constituent correspondence. Legislative files are arranged by year, with general papers followed by topical files for that year. The collection inventory, which follows, contains a detailed list of the files. Those for cities and counties usually relate to projects proposed or being implemented in those localities, such as funding sewage systems and the erection of new government buildings to serve the locality. Files regarding individuals, grouped under the heading "Persons," contain either extensive correspondence with or about the individual, or reference material. In 1957, the nation focused on events in Little Rock, Arkansas. Extensive records document the passage of civil rights bills in Congress and the reactions of Johnston's constituents and from across the country. A 1957 file on the NAACP regards Johnston's call for an investigation of the organization and suspicion that it had been subverted by the communists.[18]

EXAMPLE: Representative Henry M. Jackson Papers, University of Washington
Representative Henry M. Jackson Papers [group]
Legislative Correspondence, 1940–1952 [series]
Consists of letters between Jackson and his constituents on the legislative issues of the day, including education (Broden Bill), housing, Japanese relocation camps, public power, universal military training and un–American activities. Jackson's support of organized labor is reflected in a number of files, including those on the Taft-Hartley Act, the Fair Labor Standards Act and assorted other labor and anti-labor bills. His views on many of these legislative topics are further developed in his SPEECHES AND WRITINGS, which also often contain collected background material on a given topic.

Other locations: In the Russell B. Long papers, background files on legislation can be found in the CENTRAL FILES as well. In other collections, legislative subject files may be found in LEGISLATIVE ASSISTANTS' FILES, COMMITTEE FILES, GRANTS/PROJECTS FILES, DEPARTMENTS AND AGENCIES FILES, SPEECHES, STAFF FILES or WRITINGS AND MANUSCRIPTS. In some cases, as with Senator Long's copies of Joint Letters, letters in support of legislation signed by several senators may have been separated in the office. Senator Long's are therefore maintained as a separate sub-sub-subseries of Legislative Files.

Types of documents included: This series can include constituent correspondence, VIP correspondence, notes, telegrams, copies of research and background information and reports, copies of bills and amendments, resolutions, pages of the *Congressional Record*, committee reports, staff reports, related speeches or press releases, news clippings, Congressional Research Service reports, copies of the public law, and "other documents showing the nature and extent of the senator's participation in and the introduction and movement of bills."[19]

Arrangement: These files may arrive at the repository in one of several arrangements: by subject or congressional committee, as alphabetical central files, as alphabetical subject staff files, chronologically by year and then alphabetically within years, or as files from staff who maintain portions of legislative files based on their area of expertise. Whatever the arrangement of these files, if it is a workable system then the archives should preserve it. Only in a case where the archivist finds the system impossible to explain to researchers, such as when the arrangement of the legislative files changes frequently from year to year, should the files be rearranged. In most cases a difficult arrangement can be made accessible by computerized or manual indexes much easier than by rearrangement. Do not refolder unless folders are damaged. Remove duplicates when they are easily identified. Remove unidentified photographs.

Preservation: Since these files are likely to receive frequent research use, rebox, but do not refolder unless the folders are damaged. Only remove staples and paper clips when they show signs of deterioration. Maintain oversize material with the background files. If photographs are to remain in the files, sleeve in Mylar. If photographs are to be housed separately, insert a separation sheet. Separate audiovisual and electronic records. Remove copies of pages of the *Congressional Record* when they are on newsprint and list reference on separation sheet. Photocopy clippings if they are to be kept.

Description: Identify the types of materials included and explain the arrangement and cross reference to other legislative files in other locations. In-house finding aids could include an index using a computerized subject index, or a printed subject guide.

BILL FILES: appraised as permanent files

EXAMPLE: Senator Russell B. Long Collection, Louisiana State University

Senate Office Files [subseries]
    Legislative Files [sub-subseries]
        Bills Sponsored and Cosponsored, 1949–1986 (16 lf) [sub-sub-sub-
        series]

Includes drafts of bills, printed copies of bills, pages from the *Congressional Record*, requests from colleagues to cosponsor or support their bills, invitations from RBL to colleagues to cosponsor his bills, and status sheets on bills. These files are arranged chronologically by Congress and numerically by bill number. At the end of each Congress is a "Legislative Activities" report for RBL prepared by the Senate Computer Center, Office of the Sergeant-at-Arms, and the Committee on Rules and Administration. The report contains a subject cross-reference to bills sponsored and cosponsored by RBL and notes by his staff.

EXAMPLE: Senator Mike Gravel Papers, University of Alaska–Fairbanks
    Senator Mike Gravel Papers [group]
        Legislative [subgroup]
            Legislative Files, 1969–1980 (39 document boxes, 16 lf) Chronologically arranged [series]
            Sponsorship and Cosponsorship Notebooks [subseries]

Contains notebooks that were maintained by Gravel's office for the 92nd through the 96th Congresses. The notebooks, which are very useful and complete, do not contain the actual text of any bill, but do contain the name and number of each bill, the date it was introduced, a list of the sponsors and cosponsors, and a brief summary of the contents of the bill. In some cases the path of the bill through Congress is also traced. The format of these notebooks remains the same throughout Gravel's tenure in office, making it relatively easy to trace his legislative involvement. The notebooks are arranged chronologically and are labeled with date and content notes.

Other locations: Copies of bills might be found in almost any series. Staff might file copies for reference in their work. The personal secretary might keep copies for the Member's reference. Copies of bills sponsored by the Member will be found in the LEGISLATIVE ASSISTANTS' FILES and LEGISLATIVE SUBJECT (TOPICAL) FILES AND BACKGROUND RESEARCH, as well as in various COMMITTEE FILES and SPEECH FILES.

Types of documents included: Paul divides these files into the four categories of 1) bills individually sponsored/cosponsored; 2) proposed bills agreed to, pending or introduced; 3) proposed bills rejected by Member; and 4) bills in which Member is interested but not involved.[20] These files will, of course, contain copies of bills, amendments, and resolutions as well as committee prints and legislative histories. Other types of documents that might be found in the BILL FILE are: joint letters, those signed by several Members regarding the support or opposition of a particular bill; conference or committee reports; staff memos; speeches and press releases; bill summaries; and correspondence from agencies and executive branch; as well as background material such as Congressional Research Service reports. Offices might retain constituent correspondence regarding a specific bill in the BILL FILE. Some archivists will have appraised "pending bills" files with which the member is involved and "proposed bills rejected" as "permanent". If these appear in the BILL FILE, arrange consistently with the bills sponsored/co-sponsored files.

Arrangement: Organization can be chronologically by Congress and numerically by bill number, by subject, or by congressional committee. Arrangement of these files is possibly one of the simplest. If the BILL FILE is found chronologically at the end of each year's legislative file, it can remain there. However, for consistency with other congressional files, it would be best to separate the BILL FILE from each year and pull all years together as a complete set. This will aid removal of duplicates, simplify description, and assist researchers using such files. If the office has not followed records management guidelines and eliminated those files pertaining to bills in which the member was not involved, eliminate them at this point. Keep a list of such files eliminated.

Preservation: Copies of bills, amendments, resolutions and committee prints may be on low grade paper used by the Congress for printing such items. Many times these copies contain numerous staples. Do not photocopy nor remove staples. Pages from the *Congressional Record* that are on newsprint should be photocopied if they are to be retained. Since the paper is already of poor quality, do not refolder unless folders are damaged. If the files contain extensive VIP correspondence, then refoldering and segregation of poor paper should be considered.

Description: Explain contents and describe filing method. If bills are filed by bill number, a cross reference to the title of the bill is useful and vice versa.

LEGISLATIVE ASSISTANTS' FILES: appraised as permanent with careful weeding recommended

STAFF PROJECT FILES: appraised as permanent with careful weeding recommended

EXAMPLE: Senator Russell B. Long Collection, Louisiana State University
Senate Office files [sub-series]
    Legislative Director's Files, 1982–1986 (8 lf) [sub-subseries]
    In 1982, the position of Legislative Director was established in RBL's
office. These files represent the activities of the Legislative Director and
include research files; bills and amendments; correspondence with constituents, VIPs and agencies; notes; subject files; and committee files. Subjects include budget, Commerce Committee, Superfund, TV in the Senate,
and Transportation.

    Legislative Assistants' Files, 1960-1982 (8 lf) [sub-subseries]
    Most legislative assistants' files are in the Legislative Files or the Cen-
tral Files; however, some assistants kept extensive files of their own which
are included in this series. Files include reference materials, speech drafts,
press releases, bills, correspondence to and from RBL, and some Finance
Committee files. Each assistant's files are grouped under the individual's
name and filed alphabetically by subject. Each folder is labeled with the initials of the Legislative Assistant. An office personnel list is available in the
repository. Tax bill mark-up conference files for 1984 are restricted until
2001.
    SEE ALSO: RBL Central Files

EXAMPLE: Senator Mike Gravel Papers, University of Alaska–Fairbanks
Senator Mike Gravel Papers [group]
    Staff files [subgroup]
        Richard Aks and Mark Boyer: Staff Files, 1977–1980 (27 document
        boxes, 11 lf) Alphabetically arranged. Box 867 is restricted. [series]
    Richard Aks and Mark Boyer were members of Senator Gravel's leg-
islative research staff for several years during the Senator's second term of
office. According to a 1977 list of areas of responsibility assigned to the legislative staff, they were responsible for separate legislative concerns. However, they evidently kept their files together and frequently worked together.
Since the files were completely intermingled, no attempt has been made to
divide them into two separate sets of staff files. Richard Aks was primarily
responsible for social justice and community development issues. Mark
Boyer's areas of responsibility were Indian policy, small and regulatory agencies, and, at least for awhile, education, though at some point this became
one of Nancy MacWood's areas of responsibility. The legislative research
files of Aks and Boyer are strongest in the areas of education and community development. Additionally, there are some files which touch on issues

of social justice, such as criminal code revision, grand jury reform, and libel law. There is also a small amount of documentation of the Small Business Administration's involvement with minority contractors in Alaska, and some information dealing with proposed regulatory reform. The Aks-Boyer series is not broken down into subseries. It is arranged alphabetically by subject. Researchers interested in the issues which Aks and Boyer handled should also consult the files of staff members Nancy MacWood, Paige Bryan, and Mark Mayo for related information.

Other locations: CENTRAL FILES, ADMINISTRATIVE ASSIS-TANTS' FILES, PERSONAL SECRETARIES' FILES, LEGISLATIVE FILES or PRESS FILES.

Types of documents included: LEGISLATIVE ASSISTANTS' FILES may include correspondence, memos, reports, copies of bills and amendments, committee prints, research files, near-print materials from organizations and lobbyists, CRS reports, staff position papers, briefing memos, photographs, audiovisual recordings, and telephone logs and memos. Related items documenting the Member's "participation in the introduction and movement of bills, his/her general legislative interest, impact, and influence, as well as the interaction of legislative concerns and interest with the pressures of his/her constituency" should be present in these files. Hopefully, they also "document the development of policy positions and legislative initiatives by the legislative staff."[21]

STAFF PROJECT FILES (other than those retained by LAs) may be those retained by other professional staff such as temporarily assigned employees, fellows, or interns. Such staff may be compiling detailed studies relating to:

> a legislative, political, economic, foreign policy or other issue. Typical papers include documents authorizing the project, such as a note from the member or a memo of a conversation with the member describing its scope, purpose, objectives and/or methodology; documents created or received during the course of the project; a final report, legislative proposal or other document that signifies the completion of the project; and intermediate progress reports showing stages of development.[22]

Of course, the types of files and the content of files of the Legislative Assistants depend on the overall filing system of the office. Usually when an office has a centralized file system, Legislative Assistants only keep research and pending files in their offices. Correspondence and memos will be filed in the CENTRAL FILES. Aronsson states that LAs working in offices with centralized filing systems might keep chronological files of their memos and copies of important correspondence. Files kept by LAs could contain correspondence, memos, notes of meetings with lobbyists and other people and from hearings attended, copies of speeches they wrote, and their research files. Such LAs files will reflect the interests of the LA and of the person they work for.[23]

These files may also contain bulky publications or printed items from various organizations, lobbyists, pressure groups and individuals. Because much of this material can be found in few other places, it usually should be kept, or if not, transferred to the repository's library. A subject and author list should be kept of the materials transferred.

Arrangement: Speeches and drafts of appropriate responses to large volumes of single issue mail may be filed separately. LA files may come to the repository arranged by subjects under general issues (agriculture, defense, etc.), then subdivided alphabetically by legislation and project name. Some other LAs may arrange their files by legislative bill number. Paul recommends that: "Staff project files can be arranged in date sequence in one or more folders with proper dates and titles, for large files with more than three folders arrange by subject headings: transitory papers, authorizations, correspondence with interested parties, reference or background data and summaries, reports and final summary."[24]

When LA files arrive in this type of excellent order, little more archival arrangement is needed. The example shown from the Gravel Papers illustrates that when files are too difficult to rearrange, it is possible to keep them as they are with a proper description. Prepare separation sheets for items removed.

Preservation: The greatest difficulty with these files is their bulk and the various types of materials contained. Some research items may be printed publications that should be kept in the file but which are printed or photocopied onto very poor quality paper. Because these files are so very valuable for research, the repository should consider doing any preservation work necessary. Photocopy poor quality paper. Refolder and rebox. Enclose photographs in Mylar if they are to be kept within the files. Remove audiovisual materials and prepare separation sheets.

Description: In the series description, thoroughly but succinctly describe the overall files kept. What is in the files and how did the legislative assistants maintain their files in the office? This series needs a computerized or paper index with cross references for in-house researcher use.

SUBJECT/TOPICAL/SPECIAL INTEREST TO MEMBER OF CONGRESS: appraised as permanent with careful weeding recommended

EXAMPLE: Senator Russell B. Long Collection, Louisiana State University
Special Issues Files, 1941–1986 (17 lf) [sub-subseries]
Tidelands, 1947–1975 (5 lf) [sub-sub-subseries]
Alphabetical by topic, includes correspondence with constituents regarding tidelands in Louisiana, agency reports and correspondence, Senate hearings transcripts of testimony, reprints of bills and laws, legislative histories, legislative research materials, and staff working files.

Civil Rights Files, 1941–1971 (5 lf) [sub-sub-subseries]
Includes speeches, committee reports, press releases, research files, copies of bills, newspaper clippings, pages from the *Congressional Record*, and correspondence. Subjects include voting rights, Civil Rights bills, crime and violence, school integration, court decisions in Louisiana, and Senate Cloture.

Employee Stock Ownership Plan (ESOPs), 1965-1978 (5 lf) [sub-sub-subseries]
RBL was a proponent of ESOP. These files include correspondence with agencies, constituents, VIPs and lobbyists; research and background files; bills; and files on Banger & Co. and Louis O. Kelso, ESOP consultants.

TV in the Senate, 1960–1986 (1.5 lf) [sub-sub-subseries]
RBL was opposed to TV in the Senate. Files include speeches, background files, and correspondence.

Lt. William L. Calley, Jr., Trial, 1971 (3 inches) [sub-sub-subseries]
These files are constituent correspondence and constituent petitions in support and in opposition to the verdict at Calley's trail.

Panama Canal Treaties, 1978 (1 inch) [sub-sub-subseries]
Constituent correspondence in support and in opposition to the treaties.

EXAMPLE: Senator Mike Gravel Papers, University of Alaska–Fairbanks
Mike Gravel Papers [group]
Issue Files [subgroup]
Nuclear Energy and Weapons, 1969–1970 and 1977–1980. (7 document boxes, 3 lf) Topically arranged. [series]
Even before entering the Senate, Gravel was aware of the dangers of nuclear weapons and was determined to do what he could to halt indiscriminate nuclear testing. This series documents that concern. The bulk of it, in boxes 595–600, deals with Gravel's 1969–1970 opposition to the

underground testing of nuclear weapons, particularly in the Arctic. Contents of the series include source information and suggested revisions and changes for a "Nuclear Energy Redbook," evidently compiled by Gravel's staff member Egan O'Connor very early in Gravel's first term of office. Also in the series are reports, newspaper clippings, and correspondence on underground testing of nuclear weapons in general and on the Cannikan test on Amchitka Island. Box 601 contains proposed 1979 amendments to the Nuclear Regulatory Commission Authorization Act and to 1979 nuclear nonproliferation legislation. There is also a proposal to denuclearize the Arctic written in 1978 for the Inuit Circumpolar Conference and some information on a 1977 Gravel trip to Japan during which Gravel spoke frequently about the dangers of nuclear weapons. The series is arranged according to subject, with materials on the same subject grouped together. The folder titles listed in the container list provide the best subject guide to the materials in the series.

Alaska General Stock Ownership Corporation, 1977–1980 (2 document boxes, 2 lf) Alphabetically arranged. [series]

This series contains developmental plans and promotional materials concerning Gravel's idea to establish the Alaska General Stock Ownership Corporation. This corporation was to be the vehicle which would allow all Alaskans to share in the wealth generated by development of Alaska's natural resources, primarily oil. There is a small amount of correspondence concerning the proposed corporation and a copy of a report to the Alaska State Legislature by Louis O. Kelso, a principal architect of the proposed corporation, entitled "Design of an Alaskan General Stock Ownership Plan." Arrangement is alphabetical by subject, except that the Kelso report is boxed separately. More information on AGSOC can be found in the staff files of Jerry Gauche, William Hoffman, and Tyler F. Jones.

Types of documents included: This series can include correspondence, reports, staff memos, newsclippings, photographs, audiovisual recordings, print and near-print items, telephone logs, public opinion polls, copies of bills, background and research files, committee prints, committee hearings transcripts, pages from the *Congressional Record* and petitions.

Other locations: In many collections these files are found in LEGISLATIVE ASSISTANTS' FILES or LEGISLATIVE SUBJECT (TOPICAL) FILES AND BACKGROUND RESEARCH as well as STAFF PROJECT FILES. In the Russell Long Collection, files on these various topics can also be found in LEGISLATIVE ASSISTANTS' FILES and CENTRAL FILES.

Arrangement: These files may have a number of arrangements in the offices. They can be chronological by year or by Congress; alphabetical by subject, person's name, committee name or title of legislation; or a mixture of the two. Maintain the original filing order from the office if it does not impede research. Because of the importance to the member of these files, they should be arranged at the same level as LEGISLATIVE ASSISTANTS' FILES. If these files completely duplicate files found in the legislative assistants' files, the archivist may wish to discard them. List the title of any files discarded under the heading, SUBJECT/TOPICAL/SPECIAL INTEREST TO MEMBER OF CONGRESS, and cross reference where the duplicate file can be found. If duplicate files in this series are to be kept, it is not necessary to refolder and rebox them.

Preservation: Again, because of the importance of these files, unless they are completely duplicated elsewhere, they should receive the same level of preservation as LEGISLATIVE ASSISTANTS' FILES.

Description: The description of this series for the finding aids should be as complete as that for the LEGISLATIVE ASSISTANTS' FILES.

BRIEFING BOOKS: the copy used by the senator or representative is appraised as permanent

EXAMPLE: Senator Frank Church Papers, Boise State University
  Frank Church Papers [group]
    Public Relations (64 boxes and 42 volumes) [series]
      Issue Books [subseries]
Scrapbook style arrangement filled with clippings, notes, and pages of the *Congressional Record*. They seem to be a quick reference record of the Senator's stand on specific issues. An outstanding feature of the Issue Books, one that distinguishes them, was the number of speeches and speech drafts they contained. For ease of access, Issue Books have been transferred from their oversize loose-leaf notebooks to archival boxes.

Other locations: BRIEFING BOOKS and briefing materials can also be found in PERSONAL SECRETARIES' FILES, ADMINISTRATIVE ASSISTANTS' FILES, LEGISLATIVE ASSISTANTS' FILES, LEGISLATIVE SUBJECT (TOPICAL) FILES AND BACKGROUND RESEARCH, STAFF PROJECT FILES, BILLS FILES or PUBLIC RELATIONS FILES.

Types of documents included: These can be loose-leaf binders that the legislative staff has put together for the member's review. They might contain:

memos from staff regarding scheduled events, staff position papers, agendas, newsclippings, pages from the *Congressional Record*, speeches, and other materials pertinent to legislation.

Arrangement: They may be arranged by subject, bill number, or chronologically by date in order to assist the member. Some members annotate these BRIEFING BOOKS and use them as a reminder or tickler file. If loose-leaf, the archivist may choose to remove the pages and folder the contents, being careful to keep the pages in the original order in which they were found in the BRIEFING BOOKS. Physical division in the folders can follow the arrangement of the BRIEFING BOOKS — by Congress, then by bill number, subject, or chronology. Discard binders unless they have some notations written on them, or photocopy notes and add to the beginning or end of the file of pages from the book.

Preservation: If the decision is made to physically maintain the pages in the loose-leaf binder, the archivist must be sure to review for any conservation problems or potential loss of torn pages. Any clippings or materials on poor quality paper should be photocopied.

Description: What do they contain and what was their original purpose? Are they originals or photocopies? Cross reference to other appropriate series.

VOTING/ATTENDANCE RECORDS: appraised as permanent

EXAMPLE: Senator Russell B. Long Collection, Louisiana State University
    Legislative Files [sub-subseries]
        Voting Records, 1933–1986 (12 lf)
            [sub-sub-subseries]

Indicate how RBL voted on each bill that came before the Senate. Includes copies of bills, pages from the *Congressional Record*, printed vote tally lists, status sheets on bills, and notes by staff. These are arranged by Congress and then numerically by bill number. At the end of each Congress is a "Legislative Activities" report for RBL which gives a subject cross reference of bills sponsored and cosponsored by RBL. Included are multi-year issue indexes to Senate votes and reference materials.

EXAMPLE: Senator Mike Gravel Papers, University of Alaska–Fairbanks
    Mike Gravel Papers [group]
        Legislative [subgroup]
            Legislative Files, 1969–1980 (39 document boxes, 16 lf) Chronologically arranged. [series]
                Voting Records [subseries]

Voting Records contain both official voting records published by various governmental entities and the more informal voting records compiled in various formats from time to time by Gravel's staff. There was, unfortunately, no consistency in the way voting records were kept from year to year, so Gravel's voting record exists in these files in a form that is fragmentary and difficult to trace. The information is arranged roughly in chronological order and labeled by date.

Roll Call Votes, 1969–1980 (6 record center boxes, 8 lf). Chronologically arranged. [series]

This series contains six boxes of notebooks filled with the roll call votes of the U.S. Senate for the 91st–96th Congresses from 1969 to 1980. The notebooks are divided by each session of Congress. The notebooks were prepared by the Senate Democratic Policy Committee. A few of the notebooks contain memorandums to Gravel from various sources, such as his staff or the Library of Congress, on his voting record.

These individualized reports are prepared for members by the Republican and Democratic Policy Committees. In some cases they may be annotated by staff and may be filed with other materials.

Other locations: BILLS FILES, PERSONAL SECRETARIES' FILES, LEGISLATIVE ASSISTANTS' FILES or ADMINISTRATIVE ASSISTANTS' FILES.

Types of documents included: Included may be copies of bills, status and vote tally lists, notes, pages from the *Congressional Record*, reports, and memos.

Arrangement: The decision to weed materials in these files other than voting records depends on whether or not they are duplicates. In the Russell Long files, several copies of individual bills and pages from the *Congressional Record* were duplicated in other files and these were discarded. Information on all discards is kept in the accession file and on worksheets. Keep in original order and correct files for misfiling.

Preservation: Do not remove staples and paper clips unless deterioration has begun. VOTING/ATTENDANCE RECORDS should be reboxed and refoldered. Other materials need not be refoldered unless mixed in with the VOTING/ATTENDANCE RECORDS. If files are in loose-leaf notebooks, remove them and file in folders in the order they were originally kept in the notebooks. Discard notebooks unless covers are annotated. If nonduplicate bills and pages of the *Congressional Record* are to be kept, photocopy them.

Description: Describe what materials other than the voting reports are included and why. These materials are basically self-indexing if filed by Congress chronologically.

COMMITTEE FILES: appraised as permanent

Committee files should only be copies of the official committee files retained by the Center for Legislative Archives at the National Archives and Records Administration. Official committee records are governed by rules of the House and Senate. It is recommended that House committee records have restricted access for 30 years and Senate committee records for 20 years. See Rules XI and XXVI of the Rules of the House of Representatives, and Senate Rules XI and XXVI 10 (a), and S. Res 474, 96th Congress.[25]

EXAMPLE: Senator Russell B. Long Collection, Louisiana State University
   United States Senate Papers [series]
   Senate Committee Files, 1957–1986 (11 lf) [subseries]

The official records of Senate Committees are housed in the Legislative Records Center of the National Archives and Records Administration in Washington, D.C. In addition to the following committee files, other committee files can be found in the files of the Legislative Assistants, the Administrative Assistants, and the Legislative Director. [NOTE: Files are restricted for 20 years according to Senate Rules XI and XXVI 10 (a) and S. Res. 474, 96th Congress.]

Finance Committee Files, 1957–1986 (2 lf) [sub-subseries]

RBL served on the Senate Finance Committee from 1953 to 1986. Included are statements to the Finance Committee, background files, correspondence, staff memos, information sheets, agendas and calendars, reports, and subject files. Subject files include revenue sharing, 1980; the Windfall Profits Conference, 1980; social security, 1982–83; Conrail, 1985; budget reconciliation, 1985-86; and the Tax Reform Transition Rule, 1986.

Joint Committee on Taxation Files, 1973–1986 (8 lf) [sub-subseries]

These files deal mainly with tax reform and include mark-up files. Included are memos, correspondence with committee members and other Representatives and Senators, bills and resolutions, research files, and reports.

Ethics Committee, 1976–1982 (.05 lf) [sub-subseries]

Committee reports, bills and resolutions, background and research files, memos and correspondence.

EXAMPLE: Senator Olin D. T. Johnston Collection, University of South Carolina

Olin Dewitt Talmadge Johnston Collection [group]
  Legislative Files (121.25 lf) [series]
    Committee Files [subseries]
    Johnston was a member of the Post Office and Civil Service Committee throughout his tenure in the Senate and, in time, wielded significant influence over legislation affecting this area. This is evidenced by voluminous files regarding postal service and government employees. Johnston's lengthy service on the Judiciary Committee is reflected in voluminous files, 1953 to 1965. In the 1950s, Johnston chaired Judiciary's Subcommittee on Internal Security, investigating fears of communist influence in the United States government as well as in organizations such as the United Nations. In 1962, Johnston chaired a subcommittee of the Judiciary Committee which considered President Kennedy's appointment of Thurgood Marshall to the Second United States Circuit Court of Appeals. Johnston was accused of using delaying tactics to halt Marshall's confirmation. Over one inch of correspondence received from constituents and others from all across the country reflect the bitter division across America over this appointment.

EXAMPLE: Senator Frank Church Papers, Boise State University

Senator Frank Church Papers [group]
  Senate Committees (71 boxes) [series]
    Senator Church served on numerous committees and subcommittees during his four-term tenure in the U.S. Congress but not all of his committee activities were filed by his staff under the committee name. Researchers are advised to use the computer-produced indices to the collection in order to locate desired files. Church was appointed to the Foreign Relations Committee in 1959 by Lyndon B. Johnson. He served on this committee from 1959 to 1980, and became chairman of it in 1979. There are extensive files coded "Foreign Relations" which include related committee work such as the Subcommittee on Multinational Corporations. Another assignment to which Church devoted considerable attention was the Special Committee on Aging, 1967–1980, of which he became chairman in 1972. The committee assignment that gave Senator Church national exposure was his 1975 appointment as chairman of the Select Committee to Study Governmental Operations with Respect to Intelligence Activities, more commonly referred to as the Intelligence Activities Committee. There is little in the Church Papers on this subject. According to Senate rules, the files of committee

chairmen are considered official Senate records, and as such, remain with the committees until transferred to the National Archives.

Special Committee on Aging, 1959–1980 (7 boxes) [subseries]
Senator Church became chair of the Special Committee on Aging in 1971 and the bulk of the files cover the years since 1971. There is substantial correspondence with constituents and considerable material on legislative matters in these files. The papers are rich in all phases of the problems faced by the aging and cover such subjects as illness and aging, cost-of-living increases for Social Security recipients, the 1971 and 1981 White House Conference on Aging, nutrition for the elderly, elderly minorities, transportation problems of the elderly and Medicare. There is a separate folder of correspondence from President Jimmy Carter to the committee dated December 1976.

Other locations: COMMITTEE FILES may also be found in the ADMINISTRATIVE ASSISTANTS' FILES, LEGISLATIVE ASSISTANTS' FILES, or LEGISLATIVE SUBJECT (TOPICAL) FILES AND BACK-GROUND RESEARCH. In RBL, Commerce Committee files appear in the Legislative Director's files and Finance Committee files in the AD-MINISTRATIVE ASSISTANTS' FILES. Legislative Assistants sometimes are moved back and forth from committee details, where they actually work for the committee, and to legislative staffs in the Member's office. These frequent shifts in staff reporting lines can make arranging and describing COMMITTEE FILES difficult. The *Records Management Handbook for United States Senate Committees* is very helpful to repository archivists in understanding the distinctions and in properly identifying COMMITTEE FILES.

Types of documents included: Correspondence, memos from committee staff, information sheets, poll records, meeting announcements, notes, hearing transcripts, reports, and related items pertaining to the Member's work on committees and subcommittees, excluding records maintained by committee staff.

Arrangement: Separate committee files should be maintained in their original order if possible. When necessary, sort to bring all committee files together under the proper headings. In some cases these files can be under name of committee, as the example from Senator Long shows. Other times they will be originally filed under a staff member's name (as when the person was the liaison to the committee or worked for the committee at one time). Because of the confusion and blurred lines of supervision for committee staff and legislative assistants, these files should be sorted at the item level. Original committee file records which are inadvertently found in staff or Members' files should be photocopied and the original returned to NARA, the House or the Senate Committee. Do not remove publications and printed materials unless they are duplicates. Transfer publications to the library for cataloging. Insert separation sheet. Discard unidentified photographs. Paul states that for committee files a typical file arrangement is: "name of committee or subcommittee, membership, agenda/calendar, meetings, reports, correspondence and memos related to committee business. This file can be maintained as a central file, or more frequently, individual staff maintain separate sections, usually different committees or subcommittees."[26]

Preservation These files may contain research material that is oversize. Separate oversize items and flatten as necessary. Separate photographs or enclose them in Mylar. Rebox and refolder. Photocopy items on poor quality paper. Remove paper clips and staples.

Description If filed under staff Members' names, there should be a cross-reference to the name of the committee. All guides or inventories should contain a statement about the ownership of original committee files, citing the rule numbers. Describe the types of materials in the files and note any gaps. For example, if there had been no Finance Committee files in Senator Long's papers, an explanation would be needed.

Constituent Services Files

The representation function of Congress "includes activities designed to promote the views, goals and agendas of a constituency, providing constituent services, and communicating with one's constituency."[27]

ADMINISTRATIVE ASSISTANTS' FILES: appraised as permanent

EXAMPLE: Senator Russell B. Long, Louisiana State University
  Senator Russell B. Long Collection [group]
    Russell B. Long Papers [subgroup]
      United States Senate [series]
        Senate Office Files [subseries]
          Administrative Assistants' Files, 1949–1986 (5 lf) [sub-subseries]
      In RBL's office the Administrative Assistant worked very closely with

RBL on all activities. Included are memos to and from RBL; notes from RBL; VIP correspondence (including copies of transition letters from RBL to President Jimmy Carter, 1976, and President Ronald Reagan, 1980); memos to and from staff; research notes; office policy files; committee activity files; calendars and agendas for various meetings; mark-up committee files; and personal journals of the AA. The files of the last Administrative Assistant, Karen Stall, are restricted until 2001.

EXAMPLE: Senator Mike Gravel Papers, University of Alaska–Fairbanks
  Senator Mike Gravel Papers [group]
    Staff Files [subgroup]
      Heida Boucher: Staff Files, 1976–1980 (15 document boxes, 6 lf) Alphabetically arranged. Includes restricted files. Box 885 is restricted. [series]

Heida Boucher was Senator Gravel's administrative assistant during the later part of his second term of office. She was primarily involved in details of day-to-day office and staff management. She also traveled extensively for and with the Senator, particularly in Alaska, where she had a wealth of contacts. She was heavily involved in the Senator's 1980 re-election campaign, and she organized the closing of his office after his defeat in the August 1980 Democratic primary. Ms. Boucher's files reflect her responsibilities. There is a good deal of routine correspondence: thank-you's, trip arrangements, friendly reminders, etc. Several boxes contain staff memorandums, organization plans for the office, suggested filing system changes, and similar administrative matters. There are also some miscellaneous casework files that Ms. Boucher was evidently handling as well as several boxes of issue files. Issues that Ms. Boucher worked on included the possible Alaska capital move from Juneau to Willow and time zone change legislation. The container list for the series provides the best index to these materials. The series is divided into subseries by subject: 1. Campaign and Election Information, 2. Casework (restricted), 3. Congressional Committee Work and Miscellaneous Business, 4. Democratic Party, 5. General Correspondence, 6. Issues, 7. Political Appointments (restricted), 8. Office Operations (partially restricted). Subseries 8, Office Operations, which contains five boxes, is alphabetically arranged by box rather than by complete series in order to facilitate the necessary restrictions on personal material. Three subseries of this series are restricted or partially restricted: subseries 2. Casework; subseries 7. Political Appointments; and subseries 8. Office Operations.

As Gallagher states, "Members and their AAs usually communicate orally, eyeball to eyeball, and do not tend to write much because of the sensitivity of their positions."[28] Therefore, it is extremely important to process these files thoroughly when they are found with the collection.

In Senator Russell Long's office, the administrative assistant was also very involved in legislation and in work with the Finance Committee and campaign activities and the files reflect that.

Other locations: The ADMINISTRATIVE ASSISTANTS' FILES might appear in STAFF FILES or LEGISLATIVE ASSISTANTS' FILES or PERSONAL OFFICE FILES and OFFICE ADMINISTRATION FILES. In fact, Paul in the *Records Management Handbook* lists ADMINISTRATIVE ASSISTANTS' FILES under OFFICE ADMINISTRATION.

Arrangement: The ADMINISTRATIVE ASSISTANTS' FILES should be kept with very little weeding. According to Aronsson, the time taken to weed the files is not beneficial because the files are usually small. Even though some of the materials in the ADMINISTRATIVE ASSISTANTS' FILES might be duplicated in many other files in the congressional office, weeding is counterproductive. Retain original order when it exists at the file folder level. These files are usually by subject and then chronological. In Senator Long's office, the files were separated by name of the administrative assistant, filed by subject and chronologically within subject. These files should be handled at the item level, arranging documents in chronological order within files. Look for ADMINISTRATIVE ASSISTANTS' FILES that have gone astray. In the Russell Long papers, spiral bound notebook journals found in PERSONAL SECRETARIES' FILES were kept by former administrative assistants. These notebooks were identified by name of AA, dated and filed with the ADMINISTRATIVE ASSISTANTS' FILES chronologically.

Preservation: Refolder, rebox, unfold, flatten and remove paper clips, and staples. Remove oversize materials and insert separation sheets. Photocopy clippings and items on poor quality paper. Remove unidentified photographs. If identified photographs are to be retained in the files, sleeve in Mylar. Remove audiovisual materials and computer files on disks or tapes.

Description: Because of the importance of the administrative assistants' files, they should be subject indexed. A complete box and folder headings list is also needed. Thoroughly describe what files are included. If there are no administrative assistant's files in the collection, state that in the scope and content note.

GRANTS AND PROJECTS (REPORTS AND INDEXES): reports and indexes appraised as permanent—files appraised as permanent with careful weeding

AGENCY/DEPARTMENT FILES: appraised as permanent with weeding

STATE/DISTRICT FILES: appraised as permanent with careful weeding

Next to issue mail and casework files, GRANTS AND PROJECTS, AGENCY/DEPARTMENT FILES, and STATE/DISTRICT FILES are the most confusing, overlapping and hardest to arrange and describe. Appraisal for most is permanent with careful weeding except for AGENCY/DEPART-MENT FILES. These should be heavily weeded with only those files relating to the member's main interests kept permanently.

EXAMPLE: Senator Russell B. Long Collection, Louisiana State University
Senate Office files [subseries]
    U. S. Army Corps of Engineers Project Files, 1949–1979 (20 lf) [sub-subseries]
Files contain correspondence from constituents, agencies, lobbyists, and VIPs; statements from the Corps and other agencies, Corps studies and project background information; site plans and construction drawings; legislation; clippings; and resolutions. There is an alphabetical file by name of project, a general file that is chronological, and a "Parishes A-W" file.

    Special Issues Files, 1941–1986 (17 lf) [sub-subseries]
        Tidelands, 1947–1975 (5 lf) [sub-sub-subseries]
Alphabetical by topic, includes correspondence with constituents regarding tidelands in Louisiana; agency reports and correspondence; Senate hearings transcripts of testimony; reprints of bills and laws; legislative histories; legislative research materials; and staff working files.

    Louisiana State Affairs Files, 1949–1978 (47 lf) [sub-subseries]
Includes correspondence with state agencies on behalf of constituents; with organizations in Louisiana such as chambers of commerce regarding issues, invitations, and projects; constituents' correspondence regarding problems with state agencies and companies; general requests from constituents; and clippings. Files are mostly from state offices in Baton Rouge. The filing system is mixed alphabetical and chronological. See box list available in repository.

    Department and Independent Agency Files, 1949–1978 (92 lf) [sub-subseries]
These files are chronological, then alphabetical by name of agency, and

consist of requests from Louisiana constituents for RBL's assistance in their interactions with federal agencies. Files include correspondence, clippings, agency reports, bills, transcripts of hearings, and oversight and background information. After 1978, these files are included in the Central Files.

See Also: RBL CENTRAL FILES

These examples from Senator Long's papers are included in this section because they have a great deal of overlap. RBL's U.S. Army Corps of Engineers is a GRANTS/PROJECTS FILES, AGENCY/DEPARTMENT FILE, STATE/DISTRICT FILE and SUBJECT/TOPICAL/SPECIAL INTEREST FILE all at the same time. Whatever the file is titled, the description of the collection must make an intellectual connection among these. RBL's Tidelands files are all of the above, intellectually, as well as a LEGISLATIVE FILE. Most legislation passed regarding tidelands anywhere in the country would have an affect on Louisiana because of its topography.

EXAMPLE: Senator Frank Church Papers, Boise State University
Senator Frank Church Papers [group]
Federal Government, 1958–1980 (226 Boxes) [series]
The Federal Government files consist of correspondence, memoranda, studies pertaining to Idaho projects or proposed legislation or regulations, annual reports of agencies and some clippings. They are organized alphabetically by agency name.

General (3 boxes) [subseries]
The general files consist of a miscellany of issue correspondence with constituents. Each letter may deal with one issue or with a variety. These files can be used as an overview of the material contained in the Federal Government series.

Independent Agencies (54 boxes) [subseries]
The Independent Agencies of the Federal Government regulate the activities of specific segments of society. These files contain correspondence from Senator Church's constituents generated when they came into conflict with a particular agency and asked the senator's staff to intervene on their behalf.

Idaho (32 boxes) [series]
Idaho Office Files (6 boxes) [subseries]

North Idaho Office 1972–1980. Southern Idaho Office 1973–1980. Most of these files are from the office in Northern Idaho. The files concern issues germane to the region served by the office. Where the files overlapped those in the Washington office, the regional files were removed. Box 6 is all case files, closed until 1994.

EXAMPLE: Senator Mike Gravel Papers, University of Alaska–Fairbanks
  Senator Mike Gravel Papers [group]
    Constituent Services [subgroup]
      Public Works, 1976–1980 (7 document boxes, 3 lf) Alphabetically arranged. [series]

This series contains constituent and agency correspondence, environmental impact statements, and reports about public works projects in Alaska. Topics include the Clean Water Act of 1977 and Section 301(H), harbors in various communities, hydropower proposals for various locations, and several other miscellaneous folders relating to public works. For example, there are two folders that document the controversy between the City of Skagway and the Environmental Protection Agency surrounding the Skagway sewerage treatment plant. Senator Gravel served as chairman of the Water Resources Subcommittee of the Senate committee on Environment and Public Works from 1973 to 1980 and, in this capacity, was able to assist in securing numerous public works projects designed to benefit Alaskan communities. Some related materials can be found in the Energy series as well as in the staff files of Pat Pourchot, Tyler F. Jones, Mark Mayo, and Jerry Gauche.

Other locations: CENTRAL FILES, LEGISLATIVE FILES, LEGISLATIVE ASSISTANTS' FILES, PERSONAL SECRETARIES' FILES, CASE FILES, SUBJECT/TOPICAL/SPECIAL INTEREST or STAFF FILES.

Types of documents included: Constituent, state and agency officials, and VIP correspondence; studies and reports; descriptions of projects; case files; computer disks and tapes; form letter replies; copies of bills; clippings; research materials; staff working files; transcripts of hearings; lists; indexes; and applications for funds.

Arrangement: Alphabetical by name of project, agency, name of legislation or geographic location, and then chronological. If the actual files in addition to the indexes are kept, do not arrange below the folder level. Do arrange indexes at the item level.

Preservation: Only rebox and refolder indexes, not files. Only separate items in danger of destruction from exposure to files such as photographs, audiovisual items and computer files.

Description: Give a brief overview. A folder headings list can serve as the index if no other indexes are available from the office. Target the files for future re-evaluation for discarding. Give a complete description of the indexes.

MILITARY ACADEMY APPOINTMENT FILES (SERVICE ACADEMY): those not recommended — discard; those recommended — various appraisals

EXAMPLE: Senator Russell B. Long Collection, Louisiana State University
    Personal Office Files, 1948–1991 (34 lf) [sub-subseries]
        Miscellaneous Files, 1966–1982 (5 lf) [sub-sub-subseries]
            Service Academy Files, 1981–1982 (1 lf) [sub-sub-sub-subseries]
Requests from Louisiana students seeking RBL's nomination and recommendation for appointment at service academies include student files, letters of nomination, reference and some correspondence with academies. Filed by name of student. Previous to 1981, service academy files were filed with Legislative files. After 1982, these files were disposed of in Washington according to the office records management plan.

In Senator Long's files, MILITARY ACADEMY APPOINTMENT FILES were a separate file for only two years, 1981-82. Previous to 1981, the service appointment files were kept in the files of the staff member who handled such requests. Because these staff members also handled some legislative work, MILITARY ACADEMY APPOINTMENT FILES were interfiled with LEGISLATIVE FILES or LEGISLATIVE ASSISTANTS' FILES. In 1982, the staff archivists made the decision to appraise these files as nonpermanent and therefore such files were discarded in Washington after 1982. The decision was made by the repository to keep this one foot of MILITARY ACADEMY APPOINTMENT FILES because they came to the repository segregated in this way and it is a convenient way for researchers to sample how RBL's office handled such requests. Because it was not in keeping with the records management plan of the office to retain these files, the repository archivist placed them in the MISCELLANEOUS FILES of the PERSONAL OFFICE FILES.

EXAMPLE: Senator Frank Church Papers, Boise State University
    Frank Church Papers [group]
        Idaho (32 boxes) [series]

Academies, 1957–1976 (3 boxes) [subseries]

Church's nominations to the Air Force, Coast Guard, Merchant Marine, Navy and Army service academies. Only the files of nominees who were appointed and accepted were saved.

EXAMPLE: Senator Mike Gravel Papers, University of Alaska–Fairbanks

Senator Mike Gravel Papers [group]

Constituent Services [subgroup]

Service Academy Files, 1969–1980 (12 document boxes, 5 lf) Chronologically arranged. Restricted. [series]

This series contains incoming letters and copies of outgoing replies, telegrams, applications, supporting documents, and letters of reference relating to the nomination and appointment of cadets to the U.S. Air Force Academy, the U.S. Coast Guard Academy, the Merchant Marine Academy, the U.S. Military Academy, and the U.S. Naval Academy. The files contain some general information on each academy and information on all applicants, regardless of whether the candidate was successful or unsuccessful in his pursuit of an academy appointment. The files are chronologically arranged by year and then alphabetically by academy name. The individual applications for each academy within these divisions are not ordered. The material in this series is restricted.

Other locations: Academy appointment files may be found in CASE FILES since appointments are sometimes handled by caseworkers responsible for military matters. They may also be found in STAFF FILES, AGENCY/DEPARTMENT FILES, or STATE OFFICE FILES.

Types of documents: These files can include registers, correspondence, applications, notes, routing slips, and clippings.

Arrangement: If the decision is made to retain MILITARY ACADEMY APPOINTMENT FILES, do not arrange except at the folder level to correct any misfiles. The original order can be chronological and then alphabetical, or simply alphabetical. The only exception would be registers of appointments made which should be arranged at the item level and refoldered.

Preservation: Refolder registers of appointments made but not actual files. If registers are loose-leaf notebooks, remove files from the notebooks and folder, then discard the notebooks unless covers are annotated. These files will contain numerous items on poor quality paper. Because of the volume, do not photocopy. Remove and discard photographs if included. Do not remove staples or clips. Rebox registers but rebox files only if necessary to facilitate shelving, or if box is damaged.

Description: If registers of appointments are part of the series, describe how they are arranged and how they relate to the appointment process. If files are kept, give a brief explanation of what they are and what they include. Mention privacy concerns. Note that these files should be reviewed in the future for possible disposal.

CASEWORK—CASE FILES: appraisal is various (see Chapter 2 for a discussion of the appraisal of CASEWORK)

CASEWORK REPORTS AND INDEXES: appraised as permanent and should be microfilmed

EXAMPLE: Senator Olin D. T. Johnston Collection, University of South Carolina

Olin Dewitt Talmadge Johnston Papers [group]

Case Files (10.5 lf) [series]

Consists of a sample of constituent case file material gathered from the Senator's General, Miscellaneous, Black Book, and Case files. The sample reflects the efforts of Senator Johnston's office to intercede with government agencies on behalf of individual constituents seeking this assistance with the government bureaucracy. Throughout the years, Senator Johnston's office maintained the files in a variety of systems, at times interfiling them with general or legislative files, keeping them in a multi-year alphabetical arrangement, then in one year sequences, and maintaining, for a time, a separate "Black Book" series, containing files in which a satisfactory result was obtained. In sampling the original set of records, every fifteenth file was retained along with a small number of particularly thick files which might illustrate unusual activity on the part of the Senator's office. Typical files deal with social security payments, military transfers, and employment. Due to their confidential nature, access to case files is restricted to persons engaged in quantitative or similar studies. No personal information may be copied from these files. Two volumes of summary information, circa 1952 to 1954, appear to relate chiefly to efforts to assist with industrial development, noting favorable action taken to benefit communities and companies. One volume is arranged alphabetically by corporate name and identifies companies in and outside of South Carolina; the other is arranged by county, and concerns South Carolina only. These volumes are filed under Miscellany and are open to general research.

EXAMPLE: Senator Frank Church Papers, Boise State University

Frank Church Papers [group]

Federal Government, 1958–1980 (226 boxes) [series]

The Federal Government files consist of correspondence, memoranda, studies pertaining to Idaho projects or proposed legislation or regulations, annual reports of agencies and some clippings. They are organized alphabetically by agency name. A large part of the Senator's work was interceding with government agencies to cut through red tape and help constituents solve problems. Much of the correspondence in the Federal Government series deals with such problems. The 65 boxes of these "case files," mainly dealing with veterans, members of the military, and the elderly, will be closed to researchers until 1994 under the terms of Church's bequest.

EXAMPLE: Senator Mike Gravel Papers, University of Alaska–Fairbanks
Mike Gravel Papers [group]
Constituent Services [subgroup]
Alaskan Regional Field Office Files, 1975–1980 (41 document boxes, 17 lf) Arrangement varies. Restrictions apply to the case files in this series. [series]
Anchorage Field Office Files [subseries]
Case files [sub-subseries]

The case files contain copies of constituent correspondence about the particular problems and concerns of individual constituents. The problems addressed range from questions about missing social security checks to immigration assistance to relationships with government agencies. Each individual case file usually contains a case worker's report form, correspondence from a constituent, and copies of Gravel's reply to the constituent. Sometimes the problems were easily and quickly resolved, but some of the cases were very complex and the files are massive. All the case files are arranged alphabetically. All the case files are restricted because of their very personal nature.

EXAMPLE: Senator Henry M. Jackson Papers, University of Washington
Discarded Material: Most of the constituent case files were removed from the Senate papers and discarded. Approximately 10 percent of the 1980–83 case files were saved as a sample. (This was done since case files in the Warren G. Magnuson Papers are similar in subject matter, but end when Magnuson left office in 1980).

EXAMPLE: Senator Russell B. Long Collection, Louisiana State University
After 1982, the records management plan established for RBL's office scheduled casework files for destruction after two years. Therefore, casework

files after 1982 were discarded in Washington when the office closed. Case-work before 1982 can be found in AGENCY/DEPARTMENT FILES, STATE AFFAIRS FILES, and CENTRAL FILES. Reports on casework can be found in the computer Correspondence Management System reports of RBL's office.

Other locations: Casework can also be found in STAFF FILES, AGENCY/DEPARTMENT FILES, PROJECT FILES, STATE OFFICE FILES, ADMINISTRATIVE ASSISTANTS' FILES or LEGISLATIVE ASSISTANTS' FILES.

Types of documents included: These files can contain correspondence, case workers' report forms, telephone logs and memos, copies of bills, computer disks or tapes, and indexes on paper and on microfilm.

Arrangement: The indexes to the casework files should be alphabetical by name of constituent, agency, subject or legislation. The indexes might be manually produced or produced by computer. If managed by computer, the files might be arranged by computer item number. If the files are on microfilm, be sure the indexes are keyed to the film by name, subject or computer number. The indexes may also be on microfilm. Arrange paper indexes at the item level. Do not arrange case files below the box level. If the collection contains case files that resulted in legislation, rule changes, or had special interest and significance to the member, these should be arranged at the folder level and separated from routine cases.

Preservation: Microfilm should be stored in proper conditions. Rebox and refolder only indexes (or segregated special interest case files), not actual case files. Do not photocopy poor quality paper nor remove staples or paper clips.

Description: Fully describe indexes and special interest case files. Note how the indexes relate to any discarded files and what is contained in the indexes. Indexes on microfilm should key to the microfilm roll and frame number as well as to the hard copy file.[29] If routine case files are kept, describe what materials are included and explain restrictions. Index only special interest case files. Make only box lists for routine case files; no folder headings lists. Note that routine case files should be reviewed in the future for possible disposal.

ISSUE MAIL: repository archivist must appraise

ISSUE MAIL MASTER LIBRARY/LIBRARY OF FORM PARAGRAPHS: one copy is permanent

ISSUE MAIL INDEXES AND REPORTS: appraised as permanent (should be microfilmed)

EXAMPLE: Senator Mike Gravel Papers, University of Alaska–Fairbanks

Mike Gravel Papers [group]

Constituent Services [subgroup]

Alaskan Regional Field Office Files, 1975–1980 (41 document boxes, 17 lf) Arrangement varies. Restrictions apply to case files in this series. [series]

Fairbanks Field Office Files [subseries]

Issue Files [sub-subseries]

In addition to case files, each regional field office also maintained an issue file. The issue files of both Anchorage and Fairbanks deal primarily with the concerns of their respective regions and contain agency reports, environmental impact statements, constituent correspondence, and grant proposals. The Juneau issue files, which are much more extensive than those of the Anchorage and Fairbanks field offices, were set up in accordance with the numerical filing system used by the Washington, D.C. office.

EXAMPLE: Senator Frank Church Papers, Boise State University

Frank Church Papers [group]

Idaho [series]

Issues (23 boxes) [subseries]

These issues pertain to state, county and city affairs and should have been brought to the attention of local government officials. When the Church office could not intervene, a letter was written directing the correspondent to the appropriate state or municipal official. This series is a veritable cornucopia of Idaho information, albeit of a disparate nature. Includes case files.

EXAMPLE: Senator Russell Long's mass and pressure mail were kept separate in his office and, after 1982, all issue mail original letters from constituents and pressure groups was scheduled as nonarchival. Therefore, before the files were shipped to the repository, all issue mail was tossed. Had this not been tossed, the shipment would have been over 2,500 linear feet rather than the 1,000 linear feet that the repository received. ISSUE MAIL INDEXES AND REPORTS for RBL are found in the AUTOMATED CORRESPONDENCE FILES (see section on electronic records).

Other locations: ISSUE MAIL can be found in LEGISLATIVE FILES, AGENCY/DEPARTMENT FILES, STATE/DISTRICT FILES, STAFF FILES, GRANTS AND PROJECTS and in some SUBJECT/TOPICAL/ SPECIAL INTEREST FILES. Issues of special interest to the member may generate files in a LEGISLATIVE ASSISTANTS' FILES.[30]

Types of documents: This series can contain correspondence, form letter replies, reports, memos, proposals, petitions, copies of legislation, indexes, computer disks and tapes, and microfilm.

Arrangement: Some offices such as that of Senator Gravel develop a numerical filing system for ISSUE MAIL. Others depend on computer generated numbers and indexes to track the Issue Mail. The indexes to Issue Mail should be alphabetical by name of constituent, agency, subject or legislation. The indexes might be manually produced or produced by computer. If managed by computer, the files might be arranged by computer item number. If the files are on microfilm, be sure the indexes are keyed to the film by name, subject or computer number. The indexes may also be on microfilm. Arrange paper indexes at the item level. Do not arrange issue mail files below the box level. One complete set of all form paragraphs used in responding to issue mail should be retained. These should be arranged at the folder level and separated from the files. These are usually referred to as the ISSUE MAIL MASTER LIBRARY or LIBRARY OF FORM PARAGRAPHS. Form paragraphs that were superseded must also be kept and must be arranged so that it is possible to determine during what dates paragraphs were used.

Preservation: Microfilm should be stored in proper conditions. Rebox and refolder only indexes (or segregated special interest ISSUE MAIL), not actual files. Do not photocopy poor quality paper nor remove staples or paper clips.

Description: Fully describe indexes and special interest files. Note how the indexes relate to any discarded files and what is contained in the indexes. Indexes on microfilm should key to the microfilm roll and frame number as well as to the hard copy file.[31] If routine ISSUE MAIL is kept, describe what materials are included and explain restrictions. Index only special interest files. Make only box lists for routine files; no folder headings lists. Note that routine ISSUE MAIL files should be reviewed in the future for possible disposal.

Press Relations/Media Activities

PRESS FILES: Newsletters, Editorial/Columns (Op Eds), Press Releases, Speeches, Specialized mailings, Subject/Research: appraised as permanent with careful weeding recommended.

EXAMPLE: Senator Russell B. Long Collection, Louisiana State University

Press, 1948–1990 (bulk dates 1949–1986 (92.5 lf) [sub-subseries]
General, 1948–1990, undated (40 lf) [sub-sub-subseries]
Contains transcripts of press conferences and radio spots; copies of articles; speeches; interviews; press releases; correspondence with magazines, television stations, and radio stations regarding RBL's interviews and appearances; constituent correspondence regarding public statements and appearances. Often contains a chronological file of press releases with relevant copies of Senate bills, committee prints, etc. Press release folders occasionally contain copies of speeches made by Long on the same topic and at the same time. Speech files may contain a copy of "remarks prepared" for the speech; a transcript of the actual speech; and background materials, such as an outline of topics, texts of related speeches, schedules, lists of participants, and "suggested jokes."

EXAMPLE: Senator Frank Church Papers, Boise State University
Frank Church Papers [group]
Public Relations (64 boxes and 42 volumes) [series]
Press [subseries]
These files contain letters to and from the media, especially but not exclusively in Idaho. While the files cover many issues, the letters are often a response by Church to an editorial or a letter to the editor. Sometimes Church's position is presented in some detail.

Press Releases [subseries]
Releases are in chronological order. The Church staff also produced a subject index to this material.

Reprints [subseries]
Copies of articles by and about Church, copies of the newsletter issued by the Church staff and off-prints of Church addresses from the *Congressional Record.*

EXAMPLE: Senator Mike Gravel Papers, University of Alaska–Fairbanks
Mike Gravel Papers [group]
Public Relations [subgroup]
Press Releases, 1969–1980 (18 document boxes, 8 lf) Chronologically arranged. [series]
Press Release Notebooks, January 1969–February 1980 [subseries]
Consists of what were originally 27 working notebooks covering almost the entire 12 years of Mike Gravel's tenure in the U.S. Senate. The materials

were in large loose-leaf notebooks that were in very bad condition. For preservation purposes the materials have been removed from the notebooks, foldered and boxed, but all material remains in the original order. The notebooks contained some working drafts of press releases as well as final versions. There are also some texts of speeches, copies of newspaper articles, lists of radio and television media releases, and copies of newsletters to constituents. The arrangement is chronological by month and year. Many of the notebooks had press release indexes at the front of the volume which list the contents by date, subject and, if the item is a press release, by number and distribution. These indexes are foldered separately and are located at the beginning of each box.

EXAMPLE: Senator Olin D. T. Johnston Collection, University of South Carolina

Olin Dewitt Talmadge Johnston Collection [group]

Media Files, 1955–1964 (1.25 lf) [series]

Maintained by the public relations officer, consist primarily of texts of radio and television speeches along with correspondence with radio and television stations and newspapers regarding their coverage of Senator Johnston and political advertising. Separate media files also exist among Campaign Records for some campaigns. Material regarding legislation affecting the media is filed among the Legislative Files, under "Media."

Speeches, 1935–1965 (7.5 lf) [series]

Includes drafts and texts of remarks delivered by Johnston plus any extant related documentation such as invitations to speak, programs, and press releases. The majority of the speeches date between 1959 and 1964. Topics include agriculture, civil rights and integration, communism, Cuba, foreign aid, the Democratic Party, and postal affairs. Included are numerous speeches, 1959 to 1960, regarding civil rights, two speeches, 23 April 1959 and 23 October 1961, regarding women in government; several speeches, summer, 1959, regarding pornography; speeches, August to September 1959, on the visit to the United States by Nikita Khrushchev; a speech, 8 June 1961, regarding race relations and communism; speeches, June 1963, regarding the Supreme Court ruling on prayer in school; and a statement, 27 August 1963, titled — "Why I Tithe." This series also includes two speeches by Gladys Johnston — 31 August 1959 on women and happiness, and 16 May 1961 regarding South Carolina. Speeches are arranged chronologically.

Press Releases, 1948–1965 (2.5 lf) [series]

Consist chiefly of releases issued by Johnston's office, but also include drafts of releases, statements prepared but never released, and related documentation. Topics include agriculture, the textile industry, postal affairs and the construction of new postal facilities, appointments, and foreign affairs. Separate files have been retained for releases made by Mrs. Gladys Johnston and releases received from the White House. The releases are arranged chronologically.

Other locations: PRESS FILES in most offices will be segregated from other files. Even offices which maintain CENTRAL FILES will most often separate PRESS FILES. However, press materials can be located in other STAFF FILES, ADMINISTRATIVE ASSISTANTS' FILES, GRANTS/ PROJECTS FILES, STATE AFFAIRS, DEPARTMENTS AND AGENCIES, or LEGISLATIVE ASSISTANTS' FILES.

Types of documents included: newsletters, editorials, columns, press releases, speeches, specialized mailings, subject/research files, correspondence, press conference transcripts, interviews, schedules, trip files, chronological files, copies of bills and committee prints, lists, indexes, campaign materials, and invitations.

Preservation: As shown with the example from the Gravel papers, press materials can be found filed in many different ways, some of which are detrimental to the preservation of the files. When press notebooks can be taken apart, do so and file items in folders replicating the order in the notebooks. In PRESS FILES, photographs may be interfiled with other types of documents. Sleeve in Mylar those that will be kept with the files. Newsclippings should be photocopied. Pages from the *Congressional Record* that are to be kept should also be photocopied.

Arrangement: Press offices are either extremely meticulous about their files and the order of them or extremely disorganized and messy in their filing. Perhaps it is a lack of clerical support staff or just the personalities of press staff. One of the most prevalent arrangements in which press files appear is chronological. The next most popular filing scheme is by subject, alphabetically. Press files should be carefully ordered by item because notes from the congressperson and annotated partial speeches and full text speeches invariably creep into these files. Care should be taken not to lose notes and annotations. Also, press files are usually heavily filled with duplicates which need to be weeded. If item arrangement is more time-consuming than the repository can afford, then only remove the duplicates, leaving all other documents as found in the files. Do not refolder and rebox unless boxes are unusable.

Preservation: Once the repository decides how much staff time to devote to this series, then preservation steps can be taken accordingly. If all files are to be arranged at the item level, then remove clips, remove staples, photocopy poor quality paper, separate oversize items. If files are not to be arranged beyond the folder level, then only remove clips that have begun to rust and photocopy poor quality paper that is obviously damaging other materials. Identified photographs should be separated or sleeved in Mylar and unidentified photographs removed.

Description: Describe the arrangement and what weeding was done. When files have not been refoldered, archivists might wish to inform researchers that the repository staff made a conscious decision not to refolder these materials. Note any gaps and any unusual or missing materials.[32]

NEWSPAPER CLIPPINGS: appraised as permanent with careful weeding.

EXAMPLE: Senator Russell B. Long Collection, Louisiana State University
    Press, 1948–1990 (bulk dates 1949–1986) 92.5 lf [sub-subseries]
        Press Secretary's Files, 1982–1984 (1.5 lf) [sub-sub-subseries]
        Contains only photocopies of newspaper clippings reading files.

    Scrapbooks, 1947–1983 (1 lf) [sub-sub-subseries]
        In addition to clippings, a series of scrapbooks were kept by the Senator's office for a number of years. Due to their poor condition, all the scrapbooks were microfilmed by the Senate Microfilming Department. Newspaper clippings about RBL and clippings and magazine articles about RBL's family are included. Two scrapbooks were retained.

EXAMPLE: Senator Olin D. T. Johnston Collection, University of South Carolina
    Olin Dewitt Talmadge Johnston Collection [group]
        News Clippings, 1958–1964 (15 lf) [series]
        The series was maintained by the Senator to provide background information on persons, issues, and current events. Clippings are most frequently from the Columbia *State*, Charleston *News and Courier*, and Greenville *Times*. Included are extensive files on agricultural topics, the armed services, civil rights, political campaigns, education, persons, and postal issues.

EXAMPLE: Senator Frank Church Papers, Boise State University
    Frank Church Papers [group]
        Public Relations (64 boxes and 42 volumes) [series]

Clippings, 1968–November 1980 (22 boxes) [subseries]

These clippings are generally filed chronologically in annual groups and later, as the volume increased, in segments of a year. Within each chronological unit the clippings are filed by subject. The subjects changed over the years but usually consisted of files on political opponents, the incumbent governor in Idaho, general Idaho politics, op-ed materials, and issues that were of particular concern to Church such as the Panama Canal Treaty, education, water, agriculture, wilderness and Watergate. In later years, the clippings were circulated among the staff before filing for future reference.

Other locations: LEGISLATIVE FILES and CENTRAL FILES, CAMPAIGN FILES and STATE/DISTRICT FILES

Types of documents included: Clippings from newspapers and sometimes from magazines.

Arrangement: If the decision is made to keep clippings, the easiest arrangement is probably chronological. If there is no order to the clippings when received, place them in chronological order by month and year. If the dates are not on the clippings, put them in an undated file. If the clippings are in good order, have them microfilmed. If the repository cannot microfilm the clippings nor photocopy them, but must keep the originals, do not rebox or refolder. The acid from the clippings will only migrate to the archival folders and boxes.

Preservation: Microfilm large files or, if the clippings file is small, it can be photocopied. If original clippings are kept, do not refolder or rebox.

Description: Tell what the clippings files were prepared for (reading files, historical record, campaigns, etc.), and how they are organized. If clippings files are discarded, the inventory might contain a note to that effect and state how researchers can find newspaper coverage of the Member (through databases and indexes that refer them to microfilm of the newspapers).

In Russell B. Long's office, press staff clipped files from Louisiana newspapers regarding RBL. Most articles came from Baton Rouge, New Orleans and Shreveport. From 1982 through 1984, these daily clippings/reading files were photocopied in the Washington office. One copy was circulated and one copy was kept in the Press Secretary's file for the archives. After 1984, for the last two years of RBL's term in office, the practice was abandoned. Also, before 1982, clippings were circulated and then either tossed or left unfiled. Many relevant clippings can be found in series other than press in RBL's files. The Baton Rouge newspaper is available in full-text, key word searchable database since 1982, the Shreveport and the New Orleans newspapers are both indexed. All these papers are available in their entirety in LLMVC on microfilm. Therefore, large clippings files of unphotocopied newspaper clippings were not retained.

PHOTOGRAPHS, negatives and slides: identified ones are appraised as permanent

EXAMPLE: Senator Russell B. Long Collection, Louisiana State University Press [sub-subseries]
Photographs, 1912–1990 (16 lf) [sub-sub-subseries]
The majority are photographs taken by Senate photographers or taken in the Senate and at Senate functions. A subject, date and name index has been prepared for the photograph files. These files contain photographs from RBL's childhood, college days, and Senate career. Also included are photographs of family members, constituents, office staff, colleagues, and events. A photograph inventory is available in the repository.

EXAMPLE: Senator Frank Church Papers, Boise State University
Frank Church Papers [group]
The Frank Church Audio-Visual Collection [series]
The Photograph Collection [subseries]
The Frank Church photograph collection consists of approximately 1,500 photographs, slides, and negatives. The photographs are various sizes in black-and-white and color. The collection is arranged in eight major categories [sub-subseries]: 1. Campaigns, 2. Committees, 3. Family (includes early F.C. photos), 4. Portraits, 5. Public Relations, 6. Trips, 7. Miscellaneous, 8. Oversize.

EXAMPLE: Senator Mike Gravel Papers, University of Alaska–Fairbanks
Mike Gravel Papers [group]
Public Relations [subgroup]
Photographs, 1968–1980 [series]
This series contains the photographic materials in the Gravel collection. It is separated into four subseries according to format.

Negatives [subseries]
The negatives series contains three boxes of unordered negatives. Some of the sleeves that the negatives are enclosed in are numbered, but no key to the numbering system exists.

Contact sheets [subseries]

The contact sheets subseries is arranged chronologically by year in so far as possible. Many contact sheets were undated and these are placed in folders labeled "early," "mid," and "late" Senate career. Box 1 of the contact sheets subseries contains two notebooks of carefully organized and identified files of delegates to the 1972 Democratic National Convention. These shots are generally of Gravel with a particular delegate or group of delegates. The other three boxes of contact sheets are primarily public relations shots, many of the same occasion or person. There are also many of Gravel in various attitudes: at his desk, with his family, at parties, informal poses with constituents, and formal and informal speaking situations.

Photographs [subseries]

Contains four boxes of mostly 8 1/2"×11" black and white glossy photographs. There are a few informal color snapshots also. The shots are primarily publicity and public relations pictures of Gravel with other public and political figures, and photos of constituents. Many of the photographs are not identified but, where possible, individuals and events have been identified. There is a large color photograph, somewhat damaged, of Ted Stevens, Mike Gravel, Ernest Gruening and Elmer Rasmuson. A more detailed list of the photographs is in the container list for the series. The photographs are arranged alphabetically.

Slides [subseries]

Contains five notebooks of carefully organized, chronologically arranged slides. Frequently, large numbers of slides were shot of the same occasion or the same people. Consequently, there are many slides that are very repetitious and differ only slightly in the image they record. Specific information on dates and subjects of the slides in the collection can be found in the container list for this series.

Arrangement: Arrange chronologically, or alphabetically and then chronologically. All photographs found in other files may be retained in those files if preserved properly. Photographs from the files, however, may be removed to a separate photograph series or simply removed to be separately housed from the papers in the collection.

Preservation: Dozens of books and articles have been written about the preservation and conservation of photographic archives. The repository must follow its own rules and regulations regarding the extent of preservation or conservation that will be applied to congressional photographs. In the Russell

Figure 4.1. Photograph Inventory Page

Recrd Loc Box	Series	Beg_date End_date	Description
513 26	502 U.S. SENATE: Senate Offcie Files	85/00/00 85/00/00	Central Files: Environment (Superfund--Wetlands)
514 26	503 U.S. SENATE: Senate Office Files	85/00/00 85/00/00	Central Files: Fed. Property (Contracts)--Foreign Trade (Ref. Dat:
515 26	504 U.S. SENATE: Senate Office Files	85/00/00 85/00/00	Central Files: For. Trade (Ref. Data)--Grant Announce. (Statewide
516 26	505 U.S. SENATE: Senate Office Files	85/00/00 85/00/00	Central Files: Health & Safety (Medicaid)--Labor (Training)
517 26	506 U.S. SENATE: Senate Office Files	85/00/00 85/00/00	Central Files: Labor (Training)--Park & Wildlife (National)
518 26	507 U.S. SENATE: Senate Office Files	85/00/00 85/00/00	Central Files: Parks & Wildlife (Nat'l)--Pub. Relations (Nut File
519 26	508 U.S. SENATE: Senate Office Files	85/00/00 85/00/00	Central Files: Public Relations (Retirement)--Taxation (Corporate
520 26	509 U.S. SENATE: Senate Office Files	85/00/00 85/00/00	Central Files: Taxation (Credits--Pension Annuities)
521 26	510 U.S. SENATE: Senate Office Files	85/00/00 85/00/00	Central Files: Taxation (Real Estate)--Transportation (Aviation)
522 26	511 U.S. SENATE: Senate Office Files	85/00/00 85/00/00	Central Files: Transportation (Aviation--Conrail)
523 26	512 U.S. SENATE: Senate Office Files	85/00/00 85/00/00	Central Files: Transportation (Conrail--Ref.)
524 26	513 U.S. SENATE: Senate Office Files	85/00/00 85/00/00	Central Files: Transportation (Conrail (Ref)--Mass Transit)
525 26	514 U.S. SENATE: Senate Office Files	85/00/00 85/00/00	Central Files: Transportation (Mass Transit--Railroads)
526 26	515 U.S. SENATE: Senate Office Files	85/00/00 85/00/00	Central Files: Transportation (Railroads--Waterways)
527 26	516 U.S. SENATE: Senate Office Files	86/00/00 86/00/00	Central Files: Administration (RBL Personal)--Agriculture
528 26	517 U.S. SENATE: Senate Office Files	86/00/00 86/00/00	Central Files: Agriculture (Rice)--Civil Rights
529 26	518 U.S. SENATE: Senate Office Files	86/00/00 86/00/00	Central Files: Commerce--Energy (Coal)
530 26	519 U.S. SENATE: Senate Office Files	86/00/00 86/00/00	Central Files: Energy (Conservation)--Enviornoment)
531 26	520 U.S. SENATE: Senate Office Files	86/00/00 86/00/00	Central Files: Environment--Foreign Trade (Import Restrictions)
532 26	521 U.S. SENATE: Senate Office Files	86/00/00 86/00/00	Central Files: Foreign Trade (Ref. Data)--Health & Safety
533 26	522 U.S. SENATE: Senate Office Files	86/00/00 86/00/00	Central Files: Health & Safety--Indians
534 26	523 U.S. SENATE: Senate Office Files	86/00/00 86/00/00	Central Files: Indians--Private Enterprise
535 26	524 U.S. SENATE: Senate Office Files	86/00/00 86/00/00	Central Files: Private Enterprise--Taxation
536 26	525 U.S. SENATE: Senate Office Files	86/00/00 86/00/00	Central Files: Taxation (Credits--Savings Accounts)
537 26	526 U.S. SENATE: Senate Office Files	86/00/00 86/00/00	Central Files: Taxation (State Tax)--Transportation
538 26	527 U.S. SENATE: Senate Office Files	86/00/00 86/00/00	Central Files: Transportation (Coast Guard--Cure)
539 26	528 U.S. SENATE: Senate Office Files	86/00/00 86/00/00	Central Files: ransportation (Maritime--Railroads)
540 26	529 U.S. SENATE: Senate Office Files	86/00/00 86/00/00	Central Files: Transportation (Railroads--55 foot Channel)
541 26	530 U.S. SENATE: Senate Office Files		Corps. of Engr.Project Files:Algiers Lock & Canal--Army (Flooding
542 26	531 U.S. SENATE: Senate Office Files		Corps. of Engr. Proj.:Army Engr. Proj.--Atchafalaya Basin
543 26	532 U.S. SENATE: Senate Office Files		Corps. of Engr. Proj.:Atchafalaya Basin & Ship Canal--Bush Bayou
544 26	533 U.S. SENATE: Senate Office Files		Corps. of Engr. Proj.: Caddo/Bossier Port--Contracts/Awards

Reprinted with permission of the Louisiana and Lower Mississippi Valley Collections, LSU Libraries

B. Long papers, all photographs found within various files were removed and combined with the press photographs to make one photograph series. All photographs were identified in pencil on the verso of the photographs, and then each was sleeved in Mylar and housed in photograph folders and flat boxes.

Description: If the repository chooses to retain unidentified photographs within the files where placed by the office, or in a separate photograph file, it should be stated in the inventory that the researchers will encounter unidentified photographs. Sometimes researchers help the staff in identifying them. Unless a repository is willing to spend enormous amounts of staff time and money identifying unidentified photographs, the research value contained is minimal. See James Cross' article for the approach taken by one repository to identify their congressional photographs.[33] With the RBL photographs, all identified photographs were item indexed. Using a d-Base software program, an item inventory of all 4,000+ photographs within Senator Long's collection was created. Each photograph is listed by its number, date, and subject (See Figure 4.1). This is the only congressional collection that LLMVC plans to handle in such detail. Historically, the Long family has unique significance to Louisiana, which is the basis behind the extended resources spent on the RBL collection. In Louisiana senators' papers, photographs are removed from files when found there; unidentified ones are discarded, and all others are placed in Mylar in photograph folders, inside flat boxes. An inventory of board subjects and dates will be created in Word-Perfect and appended to the in-house finding aids. For Members of the House of Representatives' papers, identified photographs will be left in the files where found and sleeved in Mylar. Unidentified photographs will be discarded. There will be no separate inventory of photographs except those that comprise a separate press photographs file. Series descriptions will indicate when photographs appear within the series.[34]

RECORDINGS, TV AND RADIO, AUDIO, FILMS, VIDEO: appraised as permanent if physical condition is good and they are identified.

EXAMPLE: Senator Russell B. Long Collection, Louisiana State University Press, 1948–1990 [sub-subseries]
> Motion Picture Film, Audio, Videotape, 1949–1985 (34 lf) [sub-sub-subseries]

Throughout his Senate career, RBL was filmed and taped numerous times during press conference, during radio broadcasts to Louisiana constituents, on TV programs and at special functions. Topics include the major legislation and committee activities of RBL and Louisiana projects and problems. See inventory in the repository. (Some items may be restricted because of physical condition.)

EXAMPLE: Senator Frank Church Papers, Boise State University
Frank Church Papers [group]
    The Frank Church Audio-Visual Collection [series]
        The Video Collection (400 items) [subseries]
Films and videos in this collection range in viewing length from 10 seconds to more than an hour. There are 13 hours of footage on video tape. The remainder of the footage is on 16 mm film. The films or videos have been indexed by speakers, those spoken about, bills discussed, government agencies named, and specific historic events. Key words have also been applied to give the user the broadest possible access to the Collection. An abstract has been prepared for each piece. The Video Collection has been processed into four categories [sub-subseries]: 1. Campaigns, 2. Public Relations, 3. News Programs, 4. Biographical.

        The Audio Collection (750 items) [subseries]
As with the Video Collection, the Audio Collection has been indexed by speakers, those spoken about, bills discussed, government agencies named, and specific historic events. Key words have also been applied to give the user the broadest possible access to the Collection. A brief description has been prepared for each sound recording. The Audio Collection has been processed into five categories [sub-subseries]: 1. Campaigns, 2. Public Relations, 3. News Programs, 4. Committees, 5. Press Conferences.

EXAMPLE: Senator Mike Gravel Papers, University of Alaska–Fairbanks
Mike Gravel Papers [group]
    Public Relations [subgroup]
        Media Materials, 1957–1980 (323 items) [series]
            Films and Video Tapes (175 items) [subseries]
            Audio Tapes (148 items) [subseries]
The Media Materials series, 1957–1980, contains primarily Gravel's Senatorial campaign films, television spots, and radio spots. There are also a few spots from earlier campaigns, notably Gravel's campaign for Anchorage City Council and his reelection campaign to the Statehouse, 1964. Of particular note is the 1968 campaign promotional "A Man for the 70s." Gravel's election victory in that year is sometimes attributed to this film, which was

extensively aired across the state during the last week of the 1968 Senatorial campaign. In addition to the campaign materials, there are tape recordings and video tapes of speeches Gravel made, radio and television programs he appeared on, and radio and television programs he produced, such as "Open Line to Mike Gravel" and "This Week in Washington." There are also video tapes of constituent meetings which Gravel attended. This series also contains video tapes of some Senate hearings, usually on issues of importance to Alaska. Of particular interest is a set of 36 video tapes made in the fall of 1979 which record the hearings and the mark-up deliberations of the Senate Resource Committee on S.9, D-2 Alaska national interest lands legislation. Both Senators Mike Gravel and Ted Stevens figure prominently in these tapes. The media materials are not listed in the container list for the collection. However, there are handwritten log-in sheets which give a brief subject description of each item and information about its format.

Other locations: PERSONAL SECRETARIES' FILES, ADMINISTRATIVE ASSISTANTS' FILES, STATE OFFICE FILES, or CAMPAIGN FILES.

Types of materials included: Audio recordings on cassette tape, reel-to-reel tape, phonograph disks, dictabelts, and radio disks (pre–1960s); video recordings on VHS or Beta videotape (sizes ¾" to 2"), black-and-white or colored film (8mm, 16mm); and transcription and scripts on paper; plus associated campaign, biographical, or legislative materials.

Arrangement: Arrange either by subject and then chronologically, or chronologically with a subject cross-reference index.

Preservation: As resources of the repository permit, transfer all film and older videotape to standard VHS videotape, making one master and one use copy. Discard the originals. The preservation of the originals is not cost effective. Audio tapes should also be transferred to other tape if they are in poor condition. Refer to Paul, *Records Management Handbook*, Chapter V, for information on the care and storage of media materials.

Description: Tapes must be dated and identified by event or topic. When possible, identify people on the tape in addition to the member. A general inventory of these materials should be made.

MEDIA ACTIVITIES PLAN: appraised as permanent

Most often will find this in PRESS or STAFF FILES as well as CAMPAIGN FILES

PRESS MAILING LIST: appraised as permanent.

Other locations: STAFF FILES, CAMPAIGN FILES, or ADMINIS-
TRATIVE ASSISTANTS' FILES.

Types of materials included: Lists of names and addresses, schedules, calendar of activities, press contacts, correspondence, and scripts for interviews
or speeches. Mailing lists may be in electronic format.

Arrangement: Arrange chronologically within alphabetical subjects.
Eliminate duplicates. Arrange only at folder level.

Preservation: For electronic files, follow guidelines for electronic records.
Do not remove clips and staples from paper files unless the paper is in very
poor condition. Refolder and rebox.

Description: Date all mailing lists on paper or in electronic format. Do
not create subject indexes. Describe in broad terms.

Office Administration

STAFF INFORMATION FILES: lists of current and former staff, minutes
of staff meetings, staff directories: appraised as permanent.

EXAMPLE: Senator Frank Church Papers, Boise State University
  Frank Church Papers [group]
    Administration (74 boxes) [series]
      General (8 boxes) [subseries]
An amalgamation of office operational records mostly for the 1950s, and
incomplete files on the Church staff and interns for the same period. Included
are copies of "Multiple Letters," 1957–1960, which now would be called
ROBO's (form letters) and some unrelated subject files. Subject to further
retention review.

EXAMPLE: Senator Mike Gravel Papers, University of Alaska–Fairbanks
  Mike Gravel Papers [group]
    Office Records [subgroup]
      Office Records, 1970–1980 (4 document boxes, 2 lf) Alphabetically
      arranged. Partially restricted. [series]
        Financial and Staff Records, 1970–1980 [subseries]
The Financial and Staff Records subseries primarily contains the financial records of Gravel's office for 1979. Included are such things as canceled
checks, bank statements, bills, and expense vouchers. There is also one folder
which contains lists of staff members and explanations of their various
responsibilities. These lists are dated and cover the years from 1970 to 1980.

Most of the Financial and Staff Records subseries is arranged alphabetically by folder title, with the exception of the third box which contains copies of canceled checks. These check copies are arranged chronologically by month.

EXAMPLE: Senator Russell B. Long Collection, Louisiana State University

Found in PERSONAL SECRETARIES' FILES and at the beginning of AUTOMATED CORRESPONDENCE FILES and LEGISLATIVE FILES. Also in the in-house inventory to RBL is a list of administrative assistants and the dates they worked for RBL, and a list of former staff and their responsibilities.

Other locations: STAFF INFORMATION FILES may also be found in ADMINISTRATIVE ASSISTANTS' FILES, PERSONAL SECRETARIES' FILES, STAFF FILES, or LEGISLATIVE FILES.

Types of documents: Lists of current and former staff, personnel files and organizational charts.

Arrangement: Arrange chronologically, most recent list first, so that researchers will be able to decipher staff initials on documents. If individual staff files are to be retained, they should be arranged alphabetically. REMEMBER: PERSONNEL FILES dealing with employment, etc., should not be retained.

Preservation: Remove duplicates, photocopy items on poor quality paper, remove staples and paper clips. Refolder and rebox.

Description: Many of the other types of files may be identified only with staff initials, and these staff lists will act as keys. List the years the staff lists are available, if they are filed separately. If interfiled with other files, thoroughly identify the location. When in-house finding aids are on a database, a list of staff members and their positions would be useful to researchers and archivists.

MANUALS: Records management, personnel, operations, files, procedures, policy: appraised as permanent.

EXAMPLE: Senator Russell B. Long Collection, Louisiana State University

In RBL such records can be found in PERSONAL SECRETARIES' FILES, ADMINISTRATIVE ASSISTANTS' FILES, and STAFF FILES.

Other locations: OFFICE MANAGERS' FILES, PERSONAL SECRETARIES' FILES, ADMINISTRATIVE ASSISTANTS' FILES, LEGISLA-

TIVE DIRECTORS' FILES, PRESS FILES, STATE OFFICE FILES or STAFF FILES.

Types of documents included: Manuals that contain directives, policies, procedures and memos.

Arrangement: Maintain original of items within the manuals.

Preservation: If loose-leaf, remove pages and file in folders maintaining original order. Photocopy items on poor quality paper. Remove clips and staples.

Description: Give overview of the types of items contained and the dates.

MEMOS—POLICY AND PROCEDURES: appraised as permanent

EXAMPLE: Senator Mike Gravel Papers, University of Alaska–Fairbanks
  Mike Gravel Papers [group]
    Staff Files [subgroup]
      Heida Boucher: Staff Files, 1976–1980 [series]
        Office Operations [subseries]

Heida Boucher was Senator Gravel's administrative assistant during the later part of his second term of office. She was primarily involved in details of day-to-day office and staff management. Ms. Boucher's files reflect her responsibilities. There is a good deal of routine correspondence: thank-you's, trip arrangements, friendly reminders, etc. Several boxes contain staff memorandums, organizational plans for the office, suggested filing system changes, and similar administrative matters.

EXAMPLE: Senator Russell B. Long Collection, Louisiana State University

POLICY AND PROCEDURES MEMOS in RBL's office are found in the PERSONAL SECRETARIES' FILES, and ADMINISTRATIVE ASSISTANTS' FILES.

Other locations: STAFF FILES or STATE OFFICE FILES.

Types of documents included: Memos from the member, memos to the member, memos to and from staff, and notes from the member written on memos. Materials that document procedures in the office.

Arrangement: Chronological or alphabetical with cross-references. Maintain original order if possible. Arrange at the item level.

Preservation: Refolder and rebox. Remove clips and staples. Photocopy items on poor quality paper. Look for small notes that have been appended to memos and photocopy as necessary.

Description: Give dates and subjects. If the file is chronological, an alphabetical subject index is needed.

STAFF PERSONNEL FILES (includes interns and fellows): appraisal is various.

EXAMPLE: Senator Mike Gravel Papers, University of Alaska–Fairbanks
    Mike Gravel Papers [group]
        Office Records [subgroup]
            Office Records [series]
                Office Interns, 1978–1980 (restricted) [subseries]
The Office Interns subseries of the Office Records series contains letters of inquiry, applications, writing samples, and letters of recommendations for college and high-school students applying for short-term intern positions, usually summer, in Senator Gravel's office. There is also some general information about the intern program and the restructuring of it that took place in 1979-1980 under the direction of Gravel's administrative assistant, Heida Boucher.

Other locations: ADMINISTRATIVE ASSISTANTS' FILES, PERSONAL SECRETARIES' FILES, OFFICE MANAGERS' FILES, or STATE OFFICE FILES.

Types of documents included: Correspondence, applications, letters of recommendation, resumés, job descriptions and memos.

Arrangement: When personnel action files, financial disclosure statements, and performance appraisals are retained by the repository, then personal identifiers must be kept confidential. Most offices will not transfer such materials to the repository and, if they do, the repository should discard them. Individual personnel folders are most often filed alphabetically.

Preservation: Since it is unlikely that these files will be kept permanently or made available to researchers, do not refolder nor rebox until personal identifiers are removed, if ever.

Description: Do not index by individual name; just give an overview of the types of documents contained in the series.

TRAVEL FILES: Copies of itineraries and trip reports appraised as permanent. Routine travel files are temporary.

EXAMPLE: Senator Frank Church Papers, Boise State University
    Frank Church Papers [group]

Speeches, Articles, Trips and Meetings, 1941–1980 (41 boxes) [series]
Trip Files (20 boxes) [subseries]
Chronological file of Senatorial, personal and vacation trips taken by the Senator and his family. Trips are identified by the destination and sponsor.

Other locations: While the itineraries may be found in TRAVEL FILES, TRIP FILES under the personal office files may contain the full documentation of the Member's trips. Copies may also be found in ADMINISTRATIVE ASSISTANTS' FILES, CAMPAIGN FILES, STAFF FILES, or PRESS FILES.

Types of documents included: Printed and handwritten itineraries showing destination, arrival and departure times, and places and persons visited.

Arrangement: If the itineraries are available only in this file, correct any misfiles in the chronological or alphabetical arrangement at the item level. If they appear elsewhere, do not arrange these files below the folder level, and designate them to be reconsidered for permanent preservation at a later date.

Preservation: If the itineraries are available only in this file, refolder and rebox, remove staples and paper clips, photocopy poor quality paper. For identified photographs that are to be retained in the files, sleeve in Mylar. If the files appear elsewhere, do not refolder or rebox.

Description: If these appear in the TRAVEL FILES and nowhere else, give a complete description of what is included and full dates. If they appear elsewhere, give a brief summary noting that they will be reconsidered for permanent preservation.

NOTES

1. It is not the author's intention to give in-depth "conservation" advice. This section merely gives basic archival, rehousing and maintenance suggestions. Archivists who plan to apply "conservation" procedures should consult a professional conservator. Helpful preservation advice is available in a number of publications listed in the bibliography.

2. These series groupings are taken from Paul, *Records Management Handbook*, 19–41. Other series titles that do not appear in Paul's listings have been included, for example: PERSONAL SECRETARIES' FILES.

3. Aronsson, "Appraisal," 89.

4. Paul, *Documentation of Congress*, 22.

5. Aronsson, "Appraisal," 90.

6. Phillips and Ford, *Russell B. Long Collection Guide*. Reprinted with permission.

7. Tabbert, *Guide to the Mike Gravel Papers*, 52, reprinted with permission.

8. Hansen and Roberts, *Frank Church Papers*, 24, reprinted with permission.

9. Paul, *Records Management Handbook*, 22.

10. *Ibid.*, 108. Chapter V is an excellent explanation of preservation measures for special media.

11. Michael T. Moore, *The Jack Hightower Papers* (Waco, TX: Baylor University Political Collections, 1989, rev. 1990), 51.

12. Paul, *Records Management Handbook*, 21.

13. Aronsson, "Appraisal," 89–90.

14. Baylor University Political Collections Library, *The Sam B. Hall, Jr., Papers* (Waco, TX: Baylor University Political Collections Library, 1990), 53.

15. Harshook, "Processing Guidelines," 2.

16. Miller, "Guidelines," 1.

17. Paul, *Documentation of Congress*, 22.

18. Herbert Hartshook, "Inventory, Olin Dewitt Talmadge Johnston Papers, 1923–1965," Modern Political Collections, South Caroliniana Library, University of South Carolina, undated, 3–4.

19. Paul, *Records Management Handbook*, 24.

20. *Ibid.*, 25.

21. *Ibid.*, 27.

22. *Ibid.*, 28.

23. Aronsson, "Appraisal," 87–89.

24. Paul, *Records Management Handbook*, 27–28.

25. For further information about committee records see Karen Dawley Paul, *Records Management Handbook for United States Senate Committees*, s. Pub. 100-5 (Washington, DC: United States Senate, 1988).

26. Paul, *Records Management Handbook*, 26.

27. Paul, *Documentation of Congress*, 22.

28. Gallagher, "A Repository Archivist," 53.

29. Paul, *Records Management Handbook*, 30.

30. See Paul, *Documentation of Congress*, "The Research Use of Congressional Collections," 131–143; and the next chapter for information on sampling.

31. Paul, *Records Management Handbook*, 30.

32. For a case study involving the indexing of congressional speeches see, James Cross and Marsha McCurley, "Clemson University Thurmond Speeches Series Indexing Project," *American Archivist* 57 (Spring 1994): 352–363.

33. Cross, "The Silence of Deduction," 45–59.

34. In the spring of 1996, LLMVC received 11 photo CD-ROMs from the Senate Photo Studio containing 1,066 photographs from the office of Senator J. Bennett Johnston. This service is now offered to all of the Senators' offices. Repositories will find it necessary to provide access to such photo CDs for researchers as well as for staff through a computer with CD-ROM and Kodak Photo CD capabilities.

CHAPTER 5

Sampling and
Electronic Records

Sampling

Most congressional collections, especially those created in the 20th century, are voluminous. Even current computer technology is unlikely to lessen the volume of paper files created by congressional offices. Archives must consider ways to lessen the quantity of paper while maintaining the research value of the collections. Sampling techniques are frequently used by archivists to accomplish these goals.

Statistical sampling was probably first applied to congressional papers in the late 1960s and early 1970s, but archivists have suggested sampling for government records since 1940. One of the first articles related to the use of sampling in archives is Emmett J. Leahy, "Reduction of Public Records," in the January 1940 *American Archivist.* Leahy's article is based on his work at the National Archives where he proposed a twelve-point program, including scientific sampling, to be used in reducing government records. In 1952, Robert W. Lovett also recommended sampling to reduce the bulk of modern business records. Schellenberg included a recommendation for the use of statistical sampling to reduce large series in *Modern Archives: Principles and Techniques,* and in 1957 Paul Lewinson published his article on "Archival Sampling" in the October issue of the *American Archivist.* Archival literature contains many articles relating to use of statistical sampling as currently as 1996. Records management literature contains even more and, for a thorough understanding of statistical sampling, a review of social science literature is necessary.[1] The question remains, however, how can sampling procedures assist in the appraisal and arrangement and description of congressional papers?

Several series in congressional papers lend themselves to sampling. Sampling allows the archivist to eliminate portions of large series while maintaining examples that show the types of materials and information found in the series. Almost any series within a collection can be sampled if it is large enough. In congressional papers, the series most often sampled are issue and constituent mail, case files, and invitations.

In an unpublished study done for the Minnesota Historical Society, James K. Benson discusses the application of statistical sampling to large manuscript collections, including congressional papers. Benson states that in the archives sampling methods can be used to determine: 1) probability samples of unprocessed collections; 2) judgment samples to eliminate trivial records; 3) judgment samples for researchers; and 4) pilot samples to promote the use of collections. The first two can be used to reduce the size of congressional collections while the second two can help archivists assist researchers using large collections.[2]

Probability samples from unprocessed collections can help archivists learn the general distribution of topics within a record group (this is especially useful when no topical filing system or index exists). Such sampling is accurate and cost efficient. However, the detail revealed in a sample varies inversely with the size of the record group sampled. Because of this, Benson recommends "systematic" sampling. Systematic sampling begins with an estimate of the total number of items in the record group. Within the total number of items, choose an interval such as one-in-five. For example, if the total size of the record group is 100 boxes, choose one box out of every five to yield a sample size of 20 groups of five boxes each. Then choose a random number within the first interval (either the 1st, 2nd, 3rd, 4th or 5th box) and pull that one of every five. For example, out of the total record group of 100 boxes, pull every box number three out of every group of five, which will result in a total of 20 boxes. Thus the sample size would be 20 boxes.

Another way to sample large record groups is to view the total number of boxes as a "cluster" and to sample within the "cluster." The cluster could be 300 boxes from the series issue mail. An example of a cluster sample is to choose every tenth box (for a total of 30 boxes), pull one folder out of every 20 within the total 30 boxes (not the 20th folder in each box) and then pull the fifth letter out of each folder.

Benson states that

The total size of a probability sample which can reasonably be handled by one researcher with limited time and money is about 2,000 cases. A simple random sample of 2,000 cases from such a record group would have limited value for most research purposes because interesting subgroups (such as Irish section supervisors in Minnesota during the 1880s) would be represented in the sample by only a few cases. A researcher, therefore, would need help from the archival staff to identify divisions (usually called "strata") of the record group which are most important for the research topic so that a special sample design (such as "stratified random" sampling) could be constructed to pick up sufficient important detail while retaining "probability" characteristics.[3]

Judgment samples make it possible for archivists to eliminate trivial records. "One of the most important uses of judgment sampling is the selection of items to be preserved and destroyed because of space limitations for large collections."[4] Care should be taken to avoid destroying the quantitative research potential of the collection by sampling too narrowly. Both the overall distribution of similar items across topical categories, and the internal divisions — the "strata" — of groups of similar items should be preserved by the judgment sample. Benson suggests that major kinds of populations of items in the collections (such as personnel, land records, vouchers) be ranked in order of potential research value. The most important should be preserved totally, and less important series or files can be sampled systematically. Proper appraisal of congressional papers will identify the most important series and will eliminate the trivial (see Chapter 3). Thus appraisal and judgment sampling are used together to reduce the size of congressional papers collections.

In order to assist researchers doing work with congressional papers, archivists might suggest formulating judgment samples. Because congressional papers are so large, researchers will need to limit themselves to small parts of the total by choosing a "population" through judgment sampling at the beginning of their research, and then by also doing probability sampling on the "population" chosen.

Benson did a judgment sample on Congressman Clark MacGregor's papers. He chose to limit his population to folders of the Judiciary, Rules, and Ways and Means Committees within the "Legislation" files. Benson's objective was to study important public opinion issues such as tax reform, civil rights, and crime control. Following the topic categories on the folder labels and, assuming such labeling was consistent throughout the Legislation files, Benson eliminated minor topical files such as the Immigration and Nationality Subcommittee. His final total population was 920 folders. Then he reduced the population to all letters and petitions originating in

Minnesota, mailed from 1962–1969, dealing with major opinion issues and filed in the Judiciary, Rules, and Ways and Means Committee folders. Because mail "peaked" for a major topic like Civil Rights in 1964 and 1966, Benson chose to limit population further to two "peak" years for each major topic.

Finally, only 98 folders out of an estimated 3,300 in the entire Mac-Gregor collection were chosen for the population. Then Benson did a probability sampling to determine the final sample to be analyzed. "The selection of this target population was sufficiently rigorous, moreover, that probability sampling could be performed to analyze such matters as the geographic location, occupation, and sex of the letter writers and petitioners for each topic and year."[5]

Benson also feels that by adding quantitative descriptions to the inventories of collections, researchers can be led to potential topics for research.

Eleanor McKay found that, while item-by-item selective sampling of series in congressional papers had to be done by trained archivists, students could be taught to do random sampling. McKay found that "weeding by means of random selection allows the retention of a typical run of homogeneous records in a large series."[6]

Most repositories use some sampling methods. The University of Wyoming's American Heritage Center's *Archives and Manuscripts Processing Manual* advises the archivist to sample repetitive records so that only "a representative cross section of the documents is kept and the remainder is thrown away." A sample can be "random (retain documents selected arbitrarily throughout the group) or patterned (retain every nth record)." When the collection includes detailed summaries, then a smaller sample is kept. In the inventory, the archivist indicates what sampling technique was used and the percent of material retained.[7]

At Boise State University, a March 10, 1986, memo stated that, in processing Senator Frank Church's papers, large bodies of issue mail on the same subject were sampled when such mail greater than three inches in thickness was found. Archivists discussed the merits of sampling this issue mail and agreed that research needs could be satisfied by a representative sample of every 20th letter.[8]

Random sampling techniques were applied at the Mississippi Valley Collection of Memphis State University to the papers of Congressman George W. Grider (1965–1967) from Memphis, Tennessee. All series in the 152 cubic feet were sampled. The series were office files, closed case files, pending case file, campaign files, and legislative files. Only 20 percent of each series was retained.[9]

Case Files

Aronsson warns that sampling may create files to be permanently kept that the repository would have otherwise discarded. For example, if the archivist determines to use sampling on case files, is she thereby designating files to be kept by the repository that would normally be discarded?

> The decision about whether to sample depends on two factors. First, archivists must recognize that, in generating a sample, they are committing the repository to preserving material it would not otherwise retain — a sample of routine correspondence about issues not important to the principal of the collection. Second, the repository must have sufficient space to store this material and sufficient personnel to service it. Once archivists decide to sample, they must determine the purpose of that sample; for example, to document the range of interests expressed by constituents or to show how interest in a particular issue corresponds to a geographical region.[10]

Connell Gallagher of the University of Vermont plans to sample cases in Senator Stafford's office files. "Cases remain sealed, but the intention is to sample them heavily and to retain only the flavor of the senator's case-work together with a few "fat files" on more important issues that may have consumed a lot of staff time and effort." [11]

The "Research Use of Congressional Collections" survey conducted for the *Documentation of Congress* found that fewer than 10 percent of researchers responding used case files, but that 3 percent of those who did use case files found them "useful." Many archivists argue that, despite their confidential nature, case files should not be destroyed or sampled. Frank Mackaman argues that case files are valuable for research individually and collectively and that reducing their size will not increase use by researchers but might lower it. Paul Chestnut believes that case files in congressional and legislative papers are one of the few ways to document the needs of citizens who are less educated and who seldom express themselves. These archivists and others argue that case files should be kept and privacy maintained by requiring researchers to sign a document stating they will reveal no personal identifiers in their completed studies.[12]

The following example from the Senator Olin D. T. Johnston Collection, University of South Carolina, shows how one repository sampled various case files:

Olin T. Johnston Collection[group]
  Constituent files [subgroup]
    Consists of a sample of constituent case file material gathered from the

Senator's General, Miscellaneous, Black Book, and Case files. The sample reflects the efforts of Senator Johnston's office to intercede with government agencies on behalf of individual constituents seeking this assistance with the government bureaucracy. Throughout the years, Senator Johnston's office maintained the files in a variety of systems, at times interfiling them with general or legislative files, keeping them in a multi-year alphabetical arrangement, then in one-year sequences, and maintaining, for a time, a separate "Black Book" series, containing files in which a satisfactory result was obtained. In sampling the original set of records, every fifteenth file was retained along with a small number of particularly thick files which might illustrate unusual activity on the part of the Senator's office. Typical files deal with social security payments, military transfers, and employment. Due to their confidential nature, access to case files is restricted to persons engaged in quantitative or similar studies. No personal information may be copied from these files. Two volumes of summary information, circa 1952 to 1954, appear to relate chiefly to efforts to assist with industrial development, noting favorable action taken to benefit communities and companies. One volume is arranged alphabetically by corporate name and identifies companies in and outside of South Carolina; the other is arranged by county, and concerns South Carolina only. These volumes are filed under Miscellany and are open to general research.[13]

The appraisal guidelines established by the Minnesota Historical Society state that where feasible, sampling will be done of case files:

> which a) illustrate the "personal" aspects of governmental policy and b) relate specifically to Minnesota. For example, Congressman Vin Weber's district office kept the "agriculture and economic development" case files separate, and these were sampled to give a picture of the impact that the farm crisis and wetlands legislation had on southwestern Minnesota farmers. In addition, summary lists and statistical reports regarding casework would be retained for all offices. This appraisal approach mirrors that now suggested by the House Historical office. Given the extraordinary bulk of these records, their low research rate, and the fact that personal case files will be inaccessible for nearly a century after creation, broader retention strategies are not defensible.[14]

Casework contains little substantive information even though many researchers relish its anecdotal value. To accommodate them, Aronsson suggests that archivists retain a small sample. However, once the decision is made to keep a sample of case work, "access policies that protect the privacy of the individuals who wrote to their senators or representatives for help" must be developed in the repository.[15]

The House of Representatives' "Guidelines for the Disposition of House of Representatives Office Papers" suggests that case files which reflect a broader political importance (such as black lung disease, asbestos claims, toxic waste dumps) could be sampled or statistically described by the repository archivist.[16]

Issue Mail

Aronsson suggests that issue mail, because of its volume and repetitiveness, lends itself to sampling. She further recommends that archivists working with members still in Congress use the office computer systems to produce programs to generate statistically valid samples of the issue mail. This is feasible because most offices use automated systems to prepare the majority of their issue mail.[17]

Congressional offices often microfilm issue mail, but the film may not be usable because indexes to the film either were not created or are so poor as to make finding letters impossible. The Minnesota Historical Society will "preserve a random sample of randomly microfilmed issue mail of the Senate offices," and summaries and analysis of issue mail from any congressional office. The MHS archivists feel such microfilm will retain for illustrative purposes a selection of letters on most issues of any importance to Minnesota. Also, the MHS archivists will not retain issue mail from representatives offices, nor will they sample it.[18] Other archivists contend that "not sampling issue mail for representatives will present an uneven documentation."[19]

House "Guidelines for Disposition" state that issue mail, whether it is filed as a separate series or incorporated into legislative or agency files, or both, may be reviewed and sampled. However, archivists should retain what seems important to district or state and those issues of particular concern to the member.

Aronsson is right that issue mail presents archivists with some difficult decisions. It is important that the remaining parts of the papers received in the repository reflect the issues most important to the Member of Congress and that person's staff. Such letters "often provoke an individualized response prepared by the legislative assistant responsible for that subject area." Other issue mail comes from all over the country about general topics. Such letters will be answered by form letters of standard responses. But both categories of mail, those given an individualized response and those answered by form letter, are often integrated in the files. "While it is relatively simple for archivists to use the computer indexes to separate the two categories, they must first identify what issues fit into what category." Once the special interests issue mail which did not receive individualized responses is separated, it lends itself to sampling.[20]

In 1991, the Minnesota Historical Society sampled robo type correspondence generated by Hubert H. Humphery and his staff from 1974 through 1978. Eighteen cubic feet were retained and 264 cubic feet were discarded.

> The materials were sampled in several different ways, depending upon the quantity involved, and whether or not mass mailings of postcards or protest ballots had been received by Humphrey's office in response to a controversial issue. For example, a category might show that 10% of the entire collection was retained for the MHS collection, along with a sample (S) of a mass mailing. Alternatively, a complete (C) batch of letters — usually quite small but of critical importance might be retained. In the instances of MULTIPLE ISSUES, GET-WELL CARDS, and CONDOLENCES or group of related topics selected (non-systematically) perhaps as little as 1% of the original collection was retained, translating into 11,000 items of correspondence discarded in one category in one year alone.[21]

Also at the Minnesota Historical Society in 1991, the unprocessed robo-type correspondence from Muriel Humphrey's 1978 service as United States Senator was sampled. Archivists made a rough preliminary list of the contents of each box; organized the files by topic; retained a proportion of each topical group, based on its quantity (the larger the group, the smaller the percentage saved); retained master or sample copies of the response letters; and boxed and listed the retained files.[22]

At the Louisiana and Lower Mississippi Valley Collections of Louisiana State University, the archivists sampled the constituent correspondence of Congressman Clyde Holloway of Alexander, Louisiana, 1986–1991. Within each record center carton of correspondence, the third and seventh folders were pulled and then the 5th and 14th letter within each folder was retained as the sample. Folders which contained only postcard mass mail-ins or petitions were not included in the sample. (See Figure 5.1, Post 1976 Volume Mail Sampling Instructions, Strom Thurmond Institute)

EXAMPLES:

Senator Henry M. Jackson Papers, University of Washington
   Senator Henry M. Jackson Papers [group]
      Senate, 1964–72 [subgroup]
         Legislative Correspondence [series]

Legislative materials can be found throughout several series. Because of the large amount of Legislative Correspondence in this accession, the project archivist devised a means of sampling these files, so that only a representative number of letters regarding each bill or issue were kept. If 3 inches or less of incoming correspondence existed for an issue, all of it was kept; if 3 to 6 inches, 50 percent of it was saved; and if there were more than 6 inches only 20 percent of it was saved. The folders which have been sampled are indicated on the inventory and by a slip of paper in the file which indicates how much of the material has been retained. Copies of Jackson's responses to constituent letters were foldered together for each year. These "flexos" as they were called (after the word processing technique used to produce them) are filed at the end of the alphabetical sequence of legislative topics for each year.

Senator Henry M. Jackson Papers

Discarded Material: Most of the constituent case files were removed from the Senate papers and discarded. Approximately 10 percent of the 1980–83 case files were saved as a sample. (This was done since case files in the Warren G. Magnuson Papers are similar in subject matter but end when Magnuson left office in 1980.[23])

While sampling of large series has been widely accepted as a method of reducing size, caution must be taken by archivists. In her survey of the users of congressional papers collections published in *The Documentation of Congress*, Karen Dawley Paul determined that there was a high relative use of constituent correspondence, which most archivists have appraised as nonpermanent. Paul cautions that archivists should carefully review a collection before sampling or disposing of constituent correspondence to determine if any of the answers from the office represent originally composed answers. In the future, a decision to sample may have to be reached on an office-by-office basis to avoid eliminating responses to the constituents of a substantive nature.[24]

Electronic and Automated Records in Congressional Collections

The "Recommended Disposition: Papers of Members of U.S. House of Representatives" states that:

> It is impossible to generalize about the disposition of electronic records because each office creates and maintains these records in a different manner

Figure 5.1. Post 1976 Volume Mail Sampling Instructions

POST 1976 VOLUME MAIL SAMPLING INSTRUCTIONS

1. Combine all letters or postcards on the same topic. Then separate the letters from the postcards.

2. Break each of the above groups down into pro and con. Then separate the in-state material from the out-of-state material.

3. Note on the sampling sheet (example included) for each group the date, topic, bill number and/or name (if a piece of legislation is the topic, and this information is available), pro or con, and whether in-state or out-of-state.

4. If there are fewer than 25 letters for a topic, keep them all. Otherwise, keep one letter for every 25.

5. Letters with replies attached (yellow carbons or whatever) should be retained, unless all of these carbon copies have identical wording. In the latter case, follow #4, above, retaining **one** copy of the yellows as a reply form letter (see #6, below).

6. Retain all copies of Thurmond's form letter replies and any CMS coding sheets if present in the folder and put them in front of the folder.

7. Indicate on the sampling sheet the sampling method, the number retained and the number discarded. Make a copy of the completed sampling sheet and put it into the Volume Mail file. Put the original sampling sheet in the folder. If there should be more than one folder of material, put the sampling sheet in the first folder.

8. The contents of the folder should be as follows:

   sampling sheet
   form letter(s), if present
   all letters with carbons attached
   one/25

Reprinted with permission of the Strom Thurmond Institute, Clemson University Libraries

Figure 5.1. Post 1976 Sampling Instructions (continued)

VOLUME MAIL SAMPLING SHEET

TOPIC: DATE:

BILL NAME:
   NUMBER:

___IN-STATE   SAMPLING METHOD:

___OUT-OF-STATE

___PRO   HOW ANSWERED:

___CON

KEPT: DISCARDED:

NOTES:

VOLUME MAIL SAMPLING SHEET

TOPIC: Gun control   DATE: 1966

BILL NAME: Gun Control Act of 1967
   NUMBER: S. 2666

_X_ IN-STATE   SAMPLING METHOD:

___OUT-OF-STATE   Those with yellow carbon answers
                                     and 1/25

___PRO   HOW ANSWERED:

_X_ CON   Form letter, CMS dictionary item
                                     #750

KEPT: 6   DISCARDED: 88

NOTES:

and because the abilities of repositories to maintain and access these records differ. The worst case scenario is the office that maintains a straight chronological file, making it impossible to separate out the important materials from routine requests. In the best of circumstances the office will have hard copy of all computer generated materials and these will be appropriately filed. The decision must be made on a case-by-case basis. Convert to hard copy if repository cannot use material in electronic format. This kind of record will need constant monitoring as technological changes increase the likelihood that a greater number of future congressional records will be in an electronic format.[25]

Although the above was written in 1991, most repositories still do not have the capability to provide in-house access to electronic records received in congressional papers collections. Also, the appraisal of, and arrangement and description of, electronic records are still unstandardized.

History of Automation of Congressional Files

Karen Dawley Paul in *Records Management Handbook for United States Senators and Their Archival Repositories* devotes Chapter III to "The Management and Disposition of Electronic Records." This is the best assistance currently available for the records management of such materials. Paul discusses the systems used by Senators' offices to create electronic records as recently as 1991.

Congressional papers collections from the late 1980s and early 1990s will contain either some of the electronic record types discussed in Paul's chapter or paper files created by electronic records. However, congressional papers collections dated earlier than the 1980s will have a wide variety of automated records and files. While House of Representatives Members have had no centralized computer system they, too, have had a wide variety of automated methods for dealing with the enormous bulk of constituent correspondence received.

In the 1960s, congressional offices began to develop methods whereby individual letters did not have to be written for every constituent who wrote to Congress. Congressional staff developed form letters with interchangeable paragraphs on the topics most often written about by constituents. To keep track of the form letters and their appropriate variations, offices maintained "form letter libraries" or "master files of form letters." Automatic memory typewriters were used and some of the items they produced were known as "robos" and "flexos" or "flexies." Thus many congressional collections will contain files which are labeled robos, flexos, or flexies. However, the terms can be deceptive. One current Senator's office uses the term "flexies" to represent all constituent correspondence and responses to them, even though the term refers to a system that ceased to be used in 1976. These files from preelectronic systems may include the original letter from the constituent attached to a copy of a form letter sent to the individual along with worksheets which routed the correspondence through the congressional office. Robos, flexos, or flexies files may contain only the worksheets and form paragraphs used to answer constituent letters, with the constituent's original letter having been discarded. If constituent correspondence or issue mail is kept, it may be arranged by a computer-assigned number which results after the staff-assigned subject codes are entered into the computer-based correspondence management system.[26] Such files may contain constituent letters grouped together with a worksheet that indicates only the number of the form letter or form paragraph used to answer that group of letters with no copy of the congressional office's response letter attached. This is one reason that "master files of form letters and paragraphs" must be retained for the archives.

Aronsson warns that archivists must work with offices to develop procedures whereby a permanent master file of form letters is retained. If the office discards all copies of outdated language of the form letters, then researchers will be unable to reconstruct the actual responses. The computer tapes created by the Senate computer office contain only indexing information. Repositories should strive to retain the computer tapes, the paper or COM (computer output microfilm) indexes and reports, and the master file of form letter responses. Only by retaining these will the repository have research files that show the actual responses the congressional office sent to constituents.[27]

Around 1976, the Senate instituted the Correspondence Management System (CMS) which allowed offices to better manage their issue and constituent mail and case files. In the late 1970s and early 1980s, House and Senate offices began to use decentralized computer systems from authorized vendors that also managed issue and constituent mail, case files, routine office work, legislative files, and speech writing. Some offices later added local area network capabilities and electronic mail to their systems.[28]

For example, Senator Russell B. Long's office shows how these types of systems have been utilized:

> RBL's office used a number of different automation systems to handle constituent correspondence and issue mail. Early systems were more decentralized, but in 1982 the office began to use the centralized Correspondence Management System of the Senate Computer Center. This automated

system provides a method for creating many similar, but individualized, letters by using approved paragraphs or letters of text merged with constituent names and addresses. The major files of information available from the system include the name and address of the constituent, the aide responsible for answering the letter, at least three subject terms about the letter, a paragraph item number, the date of correspondence, and brief comments about the letter. These files contain the various reports issued by the CMS for RBL's office. The magnetic tapes of RBL's files are also available. [NOTE: According to RBL's Office Records Management Plan, constituent letters, issue mail, postcards, telegrams and letters answered by CMS were discarded in Washington after the Central Files system was established in 1979. In order to research such files, the CMS reports must be used.] Previous to CMS, decentralized automated systems were used that performed essentially the same function on a lesser scale than CMS. (Pre-1979 the system was called "Flexos"; 1979–1982 a mag card system 6 that produced "robos" was used; CMS was used from 1982 until the office closed in 1986.) A new decentralized automated system was added in 1982. This was the Honeywell Office Automation System (OAS). The records kept for the decentralized systems are similar and include the library of form letters and/or paragraphs, including those that are outdated; indexing terms and reports; and codes.[29]

Current Electronic Systems

Currently, the Senate Computer Center makes available to the offices a number of centralized systems and databases through the Senate communications network. For a thorough understanding of these systems, consult Karen Dawley Paul, *Records Management Handbook for United States Senators and their Archival Repositories*, pages 43–98. The Constituent Services System (CSS) is the system used to generate individualized letters by merging approved paragraphs with names and addresses and is most often used for answering large-volume issue mail. Offices utilize the system by linking their personal computers with the Senate network. Other separate databases are the Automated Indexing System (AIS), the Senate Mail File System, and Legislative Information System (LEGIS). Also available are two subsystems of CSS, the Casework System (CWS) and the CSS Press System.[30] From these systems, numerous management reports are available on computer output microfilm (COM) or on paper. The appraisal of these reports is covered in Paul's *Handbook*. The Senate Computer System will make available to the archival repository magnetic tapes which contain indexes to correspondence files if the repository requests them.

Since 1991, these systems have gradually been replaced by the Senate

Mail System (SMS), which is a single relational database management system. Relational databases link fields, which makes it possible for information to be accessed through many different access points. The office can locate by name, subject, date or format all the occurrences of the same event. For example, all correspondence and speeches relating to "tax reform" can be found by searching the database by that subject. Management reports continue to be available and have the same appraisal guidelines as previously produced reports.[31]

The House of Representatives offices have decentralized computer systems, as do Senate offices. The systems are usually PC (personal computer) and LAN (local area network) based, necessitating staff responsibility for proper management of electronic records. Standard conventions of naming files, making backup tapes and archival tapes, designating files as permanent or non-permanent as they are created, and overall computer understanding is imperative to establishing good archival records.[32]

As part of the decentralized LANs, congressional offices now have electronic mail (E-mail) and access to the Internet through communications software packages. Electronic mail requires files management by the staff with consideration for archival requirements. Offices should plan to maintain electronic files of electronic mail for the repository; users will tag these as archival (permanent) or non-archival (non-permanent), with the understanding that the tapes sent to the repository will contain only those messages identified as archival. Transmission data that makes E-mail messages understandable must also be preserved, along with dates, identities of senders and receivers, and any other data that is necessary for adequate documentation.[33]

Paul states that

> Decentralized systems have shifted the burden of a system's management from the Senate Computer Center to the individual office. Each office now bears primary responsibility for instituting electronic records creation and retention guidelines, developing controlled vocabularies for standardized indexing and filing, implementing procedures for transferring permanent information to an archival storage medium, and for preserving fragile computer media.[34]

Archival Management

Repository archivists need to become involved with congressional offices regarding the electronic records to be created by the offices. Early involvement by archivists will alleviate confusion about what records are being created and why. It might also prevent the loss of archival files and keep non-archival electronic files from being sent to the repository.

Repository archivists can expect to receive the following electronic records or paper or microfilm files related to electronic records from congressional offices:

1) management reports related to one of the Senate Computer Office databases either on COM or on paper;

2) electronic tapes of indexes from the Senate Computer Office;

3) management reports generated by an office decentralized system; and

4) electronic records from decentralized systems on tape or disks.

Any reports generated on paper or microfilm by the Senate Computer Office should be appraised according to the disposition guidelines in Paul's *Records Management Handbook*. Keeping reports that are not appraised as permanent can require enormous amounts of stack space. Each repository and congressional office should follow guidelines for the appraisal of series on paper form. For example, electronic records of speech files should have the same retention as speech files on paper.

Should the repository require the congressional office to make all archival files available in paper form, in electronic form (ASCII, or with software imbedded, such as WordPerfect files), or in a combination of both, or should all archival files be available in both paper and electronic format? This depends on what the repository is capable of making accessible. Electronic records are of little use in a repository which does not have computers capable of reading tapes or disks made from tapes. In fact, many repositories will not be able to convert the tapes to disks. Also needed are computers which researchers can use to access the electronic records. Few repositories have PCs that patrons can use and, even though many researchers now come to reading rooms with portable computers, do archivists really want to give them disks of congressional electronic records which researchers could then copy to their own computers? Finally, electronic tapes from the Senate Computer Office can only be read on a main frame computer and, for researchers to use it, they must have a sophisticated computer knowledge and some advanced software (such as SASS or SPSS) to gain anything from it. (In the eight years the RBL tapes have been in the LLMVC, not one researcher has asked to use them, even though it has been advertised that they are available and that mainframe time and SASS and SPSS are available for use.)

In the "Research Use of Congressional Collections" survey done for the *Documentation of Congress* report, use of electronic records as a format was not questioned. It is implied that the questions regarding use of series (legislative files, constituent/administrative files, press files, etc.) meant use of the series in any format — paper, video tape, audio tape, microfilm, or electronic. Only the use of photographs as an individual format was queried and even then there was no specification as to whether the photographic images were on paper, videotape, digital disks or microfilm. Certainly in a future survey, the research use value of various formats should be reviewed. However, the high research use of constituent services, issue mail and indexes causes one to assume that the use was done in whatever format was made available by the repository. A large number of repositories and congressional offices have their constituent and issue mail indexes output on COM. Exactly how many actually have indexes available on electronic tape is unknown and requires greater study.

Care is essential in preserving electronic records. For example, in the 1970s, the office of Congressman Silvio O. Conte of Massachusetts "adopted a computer indexing system to handle constituent correspondence." The Conte Papers' archivist at the University of Massachusetts has learned, however, that "the computer tapes were wiped out and there are no surviving hard copies of the indexes, the end result being 90 boxes of randomly filed, unfoldered, constituent correspondence."[35] The early involvement of the repository archivist in the management of the electronic records would have prevented such a disaster.

Even though a repository does not have equipment to make electronic files available to researchers at the time the congressional collection is received, the repository must plan for future possibilities and capabilities for themselves, their researchers, and congressional offices. In order to ensure that the files are useable in the future, congressional offices and repository archivists should work with the appropriate company representatives to ensure that archival electronic tapes are produced (floppy disks are not appropriate for long term storage although optical disks are now accepted by NARA). Archival tapes differ from daily system back-up tapes, and a conscious effort must be made to create such tapes as well as to provide the appropriate documentation. (In the Senate, the Senate Computer Office is prepared to assist with producing archival tapes from their systems. Approved vendors for congressional offices such as Honeywell, Data General, and Prime are also prepared to instruct offices in the procedures needed to produce archival tapes. Also, consult Paul *Handbook*, 53–57.) The *Documentation of Congress* report recommends that "standard software data bases containing documents, information files and index information should be preserved in electronic format."[36]

Computer capabilities change almost every day and it is very difficult to predict what electronic records will be available from congressional offices in the next few years. It is impossible to publish the most current information on the changes because it is out of date before it reaches print. Each repository that collects congressional papers must remain aware of the new and different uses congressional offices make of electronic systems. By working together, repositories and congressional offices can provide the electronic records necessary for future research.

NOTES

1. Emmett J. Leahy, "Reduction of Public Records," *American Archivist* 3 (January 1940): 13–38; Robert W. Lovett, "The Appraisal of Older Business Records," *American Archivist* 15 (April 1952): 231–239; Theodore R. Schellenberg, *Modern Archives: Principles and Techniques* (Chicago: University of Chicago Press, 1956); Paul Lewinson, "Archival Sampling," *American Archivist* 20 (October 1957): 308–309. See also: Frank Boles, "Sampling in Archives," *American Archivist* 44 (Spring 1982): 130; Joseph Carvalho, "Archival Application of Math Sampling," *Records Management Quarterly* 18 (January 1984): 60–62; and Lewis R. Aiken, "Sixteen Computer Programs for Selecting, Assigning, and Evaluating Samples," *Educational and Psychological Measurement* 54 (Fall 1994): 699–704.

2. James Benson, "Sampling Techniques in Archival Management and Quantitative Research," (Paper prepared for the Minnesota Historical Society, 1976), 1–4.

3. *Ibid.*, 2.

4. *Ibid.*

5. *Ibid.*

6. Eleanor McKay, "Random Sampling Techniques: A Method of Reducing Large, Homogeneous Series in Congressional Papers," *American Archivist* 41 (July 1978): 287.

7. Maxine Trost, *Archives and Manuscripts Processing Manual* (Cheyenne, WY: University of Wyoming, American Heritage Center, 1990), 6.

8. Memo, March 10, 1986, Senator Frank Church Papers Project, Boise State University.

9. McKay, "Random Sampling Techniques," 288.

10. Aronsson, "Appraising," 92.

11. Gallagher, "Repository Archivist," 50.

12. Frank Mackaman, "Managing Case Files in Congressional Collections: The Hazards of Prophecy," *Midwestern Archivist* 4 (1978): 98; Chestnut, "State Legislators," 167–168; and Margery N. Sly, "Access to Congressional Case Files: Survey of Practices, Implications for Use," unpublished, ca. 1987: 13–15.

13. Hartsook, "Inventory Olin D.T. Johnston," 4.

14. Minnesota Historical Society, "Appraisal Guidelines," 3–4.

15. Aronsson, "Appraisal," 91–92.

16. Miller, "Guidelines," 3.

17. Aronsson, "Appraisal," 91–92.

18. Minnesota Historical Society, "Appraisal Committee Report," 3–4.

19. Sheryl B. Vogt letter to the author, March 31, 1995.

20. Aronsson, "Appraisal," 91–92.

21. Minnesota Historical Society, Technical Processing Memorandum, August 14, 1991.

22. Minnesota Historical Society, Technical Processing Memorandum, February 8, 1993.

23. "Jackson Inventories" microfiche.

24. Paul, *Documentation of Congress*, 136.

25. Miller, "Guidelines," 5.

26. Paul, *Records Management Handbook*, 31.

27. Aronsson, "Appraisal," 91, 103–104.

28. At the annual meeting of the Society of American Archivists in 1994, Naomi Lynn Nelson presented a paper discussing the history of the implementation of automated systems in the United States Senate, and Brian A. Williams presented a paper on "Constituent Correspondence and CMS." Both papers are currently unpublished.

29. Phillips and Ford, *Guide to the Russell B. Long Collection*, unpaged.

30. Paul, *Records Management Handbook*, 46.

31. Contact the Senate Archivist's office for further information on the relational database. Also see Chapter 2 for information on databases used as finding aids for congressional papers.

32. Paul, *Records Management Handbook*, 53–57.

33. "Electronic Mail Systems," Appendix, 36 CFR part 1234, Electronic Records Regulations, National Archives and Records Administration, 1994; see also NARA's "Standards for Management of Federal Records Created or Received on Electronic Mail Systems," and "Managing Electronic Records Instructional Guide."

34. Paul, *Records Management Handbook*, 53.

35. Gail Giroux, "News from the University of Massachusetts," Society of American Archivists Congressional Papers Roundtable *Newsletter*, August 1994, 3.

36. Paul, *Documentation of Congress*, 5.

Collecting Policy
of the Richard B. Russell
Library for Political Research
and Studies, University
of Georgia Libraries

I. **Statement of Purpose**: The University of Georgia Libraries
    acquired the Richard B. Russell Memorial Library in 1973
    through the combined efforts of the Richard B. Russell
    Foundation, Inc., the Georgia General Assembly, and the
    University System of Georgia. Dedicated in 1974, the Russell
    Library housed the late Senator Russell's papers and those
    of Georgia congressional representatives contemporary to the
    senator and his career. In 1982, the Library's collection
    policy formally acknowledged the acquisition of the papers of
    twentieth-century Georgia politicians, elected officials,
    federal appointees, and political parties and groups.
    Holdings support research and study of politics and policy in
    Georgia and the nation.

    A department within the University of Georgia Libraries, the
    Russell Library is administratively under the Director of
    Libraries. The Russell Foundation continues to provide
    supplemental financial and advisory support to the Library.
    The University's Director of Libraries is a member of the
    Foundation's Board of Trustees, and the Russell Library
    department head makes an annual report to the Foundation.

*Reprinted with permission of the Richard B. Russell Library for Political Research and
Studies*

183

II. **Types of Programs Supported by the Collection:**

A. **Research** - The manuscripts collected and made available
will further the research of UGA faculty, students,
visiting scholars and the public in the political and
social history of the state and nation. The Russell
Library seeks to provide sources on twentieth century
political history of Georgia and the United States
Congress, achievements of individual congressmen and
other political figures, as well as materials that build
on current strengths.

B. **Preservation and Security** - Crucial to the ongoing
operation of the Russell Library program is the
preservation of research materials. The holdings
maintenance program at the Russell Library includes:
deacidification of manuscripts, encapsulation and
preservation photocopying. Materials held in the
Russell Library are non-circulating and maintained in
closed stacks. Security measures include an alarm system
that is monitored by the library security personnel.

C. **Exhibitions** - The Russell Library mounts on a rotating
basis exhibitions featuring and interpreting materials
from the collections. The exhibit area consists of free-
standing display boards, exhibit cases and an office re-
creation. Exhibits are prepared by Russell staff, under
the coordination of the head of the library. The Russell
Library will loan unrestricted materials and facsimiles
for exhibition to other research institutions when the
policies and facilities of those institutions meet
acceptable standards and proper credit is given to the
Russell Library. On occasion, library staff produce
traveling exhibits.

D. **Outreach** - The Russell Library furthers the use
and development of the collections through an outreach
program that increases public awareness of the nature
and relevance of the collections. This program includes
exhibitions (see II. C), tours of the Russell Library and
presentations by the head and staff of the Russell
library; and publications such as brochures and
bibliographies. Awareness of the collections among the
scholarly community is fostered by publicizing
acquisitions in professional publications and national
data bases. Staff members give distinct emphasis to
encourage research use by undergraduate classes through
presentations and special research projects.

E. **Acquisitions** - The Russell Library acquires
materials through donation, loan, deposit, and
purchase. Donations of materials and funds are essential
to maintaining and developing the collections. Grant
funding for special projects is sought when such
projects do not diminish the level of care and service
of the collections, and when they can contribute
substantially to the acquisition, arrangement and
description, or servicing of the collections. A small
select reference collection is purchased to supplement
research of the collections.

III. <u>**Clientele served by the Collection**</u>

    A. Scholars - University faculty and staff, faculty from other universities and others involved in original research are permitted to use the collection after proper registration.

    B. Graduate and Undergraduate students - The above applies to graduate and undergraduate students as well.

    C. Pre-college students - Pre-college students are granted use of the Russell library with proper identification and registration.

    D. General Public - Members of the general public are welcome to use the Russell Library with proper identification and registration.

IV. <u>**Priorities and Limitations of the Collection**</u>

    A. Present Collection Strengths - The Russell Library is strongest in twentieth century Georgia politics, as well as agriculture, civil rights legislation, national defense, Kennedy and Johnson Administrations, and foreign policy.

    B. Present Collecting Level - The Russell Library covers the history and politics of Georgia and the United States during the twentieth century, with emphasis on: Georgia political leaders, organizations and issues.

    C. Present identified Limitations - The Russell Library research needs include subject material relating to minorities (race, religion, and gender), republican political activity, and political journalism (cartoonists, columnists).

    D. Desired level of Collecting - As a major research center on Georgia political history, the Russell Library will exhaustively and aggressively collect materials that pertain to the political history of Georgia, as specified in IV.B and IV.C, including material written by and about Georgian political leaders, organizations and issues.

For documentation of congressional collections, the Russell Library follows guidelines recommended in *The Documentation of Congress: Report of the Congressional Archivists Roundtable Taskforce on Congressional Documentation* (Washington S. Pub. 102-20, 1992).

    E. Geographical areas Collected - Georgia.

    F. Chronological periods Collected - Mid-nineteenth century to present.

    G. Subject areas Collected - The Russell Library collects in all subject areas, as specified in IV.A, IV.B and IV.C, with particular emphasis to political history.

    H. Forms of Material Collection - In addition to manuscripts the Russell Library accepts photographs, audio-visual materials, maps, pamphlets, microform, oral history, federal and state government documents, and selected memorabilia.

J. Exclusions - The Russell Library will not generally accept the following: Materials that reflect the political history of another region or state or partial manuscripts and archival collections when major portions have already been deposited in another repository.

V. **Cooperative Agreements Affecting the Collecting Policy:** The Russell Library recognizes that other institutions collect in the same or overlapping areas, and will seek similar unique resources for their own collections. The Russell Library also recognizes that other institutions may have prior claim on such materials or be a more appropriate repository to house them. In cases where legitimate collecting interests of the Russell Library and another repository directly conflict, the Russell Library will use the best interest of the scholarly community as a criterion in pursuing a resolution.

VI. **Statement of Deaccessioning Policy:** Duplicates and materials that do not reflect the collecting areas of the Russell Library may be deaccessioned, subject to the terms of acquisitions, and state and federal laws, and offered to other more appropriate institutions or the donor or donor's family.

VII. **Procedures Affecting Collecting Policy and Its Expedition:**

A. **Deed of Gift -** The Russell Library does not accept materials without a legal transfer of title, deed of gift, or other official acknowledgment.

B. **Loans and Deposits:** Materials loaned to or deposited with the Russell Library are accepted when the conditions for acceptance are favorable to the UGA libraries.

C. **Closed Collections -** The Russell Library does not accept manuscript collections that are closed for perpetuity.

D. **Deaccessioning -** The Russell Library reserves the right to deaccession any materials within its collections, subject to the terms of acquisition and the notification of the donor or his/her heirs.

E. **Exhibitions -** The Russell Library reserves the right to include unrestricted materials in exhibitions, in accordance with normally accepted archival principles and practices.

F. **Revision of Policies -** The Russell Library reserves the right to change the preceding policies.

VIII. **Procedures for Monitoring Development and Reviewing Collection Development Guidelines:** This collecting policy is designed to meet the goals of the UGA Libraries and the Russell Library. In order to determine the effectiveness of the collecting policy, the staff will review the acquisitions, user records, and deaccessions occurring under these policies to detect any needed changes. Every five years the policy will be re-evaluated and changed as needed to meet the continuing goals of the UGA Libraries and the Russell Library.

Bibliography

Aiken, Lewis R. "Sixteen Computer Programs for Selecting, Assigning, and Evaluating Samples." *Education and Psychological Measurement* 54 (Fall 1994): 699–704.

American Library Association and the Society of American Archivists." Joint Statement on Access to Original Materials in Libraries, Archives, and Manuscripts Repositories." *Archival Outlook* (July 1993): 14–15.

Aronsson, Patricia. "Appraisal of Twentieth-Century Congressional Collections." *Archival Choices: Managing the Historical Record in an Age of Abundance.* Editor, Nancy E. Peace. Lexington, MA: D.C. Heath, 1984. 81–104.

Baker, Richard. "Managing Congressional Papers: A View of the Senate." *American Archivist* 41 (July 1978): 291–296.

Baylor Political Collections Library. *The Sam B. Hall, Jr. Papers.* Waco, TX: Baylor University, 1990.

Becker, Ronald L. "On Deposit: A Handshake and a Lawsuit." *American Archivist* 56 (Spring 1993): 320–328.

Bellardo, Lewis J., and Lynn Lady Bellardo. *A Glossary for Archivists, Manuscript Curators, and Records Managers.* Archival Fundamental Series. Chicago: Society of American Archivists, 1992.

Benson, James K. "Sampling Techniques in Archival Management and Quantitative Research." Unpublished report prepared for the Minnesota Historical Society, Summer 1976.

Boles, Frank. "Disrespecting Original Order." *American Archivist* 45 (Winter 1982): 26–32.

————. "Sampling in Archives." *American Archivist* 44 (Spring 1981): 125-130.

Caldwell, John M., and John R. Lovett, Jr. "Photographic Collections and Congressional History." *Extensions* (Fall 1986): 12.

Cameron, Ross. "Appraisal Strategies for Machine Readable Case Files." *Provenance* 1 (Spring 1983): 50–69.

Carvalho, Joseph. "Archival Application of Math Sampling." *Records Management Quarterly* 18 (January 1984): 60–62.

Chestnut, Paul I. "Appraising the Papers of State Legislators," *American Archivist* 48 (1985): 167–178.

Cross, James Edward. "The Science of Deduction: Dating and Identifying Photographs in Twentieth Century Political Collections." *Provenance* 6 (Spring 1988): 45–59.

_____ and Marsha McCurley. "Clemson University Thurmond Speeches Series Indexing Project." *American Archivist* 57 (Spring 1994): 352–363.

Gallagher, Connell B. "A Repository Archivist on Capitol Hill." *The Midwestern Archivist* 16 (1991): 49–58.

Galloway, Edward. "News from Carneige-Mellon University — The Heinz Archives." Society of American Archivists Congressional Papers Roundtable *Newsletter* (November 1994): 4–5.

Getty Art History Information Program. *Art and Architecture Thesaurus (AAT)*. New York: Oxford University Press, 1990.

Giroux, Gail. "News from the University of Massachusetts." Society of American Archivists Congressional Papers Roundtable *Newsletter* (August 1994): 3.

Gorman, Michael, and Paul W. Winker, eds. *Anglo-American Cataloguing Rules*, 2nd ed., revised. Chicago: American Library Association, 1988.

Greene, Mark. "Appraisal of Congressional Records at the Minnesota Historical Society: A Case Study." *Archival Issues* 19 (Winter 1994): 31–43.

Ham, Gerald. *Appraising Archives and Manuscripts*. Chicago: Society of American Archivists, 1992.

Hansen, Ralph W., and Deborah J. Roberts. *The Frank Church Papers*. Boise, ID: Boise State University Library, 1988.

Hartsook, Herbert. "Inventory, Olin Dewitt Talmadge Johnston Papers, 1923–1965." Modern Political Collections, South Caroliniana Library, University of South Carolina, 1990.

_____. "Processing Guidelines," Modern Political Collections, South Caroliniana Library, University of South Carolina, 1992.

"Henry M. Jackson Papers Inventories." Manuscripts Department, University of Washington Libraries, 1989.

Henson, Steven L. *Archives, Personal Papers and Manuscripts: A Cataloging Manual for Archival Repositories, Historical Societies and Manuscript Libraries*. 2nd ed. Chicago: Society of American Archivists, 1989.

Holmes, Oliver W. "Archival Arrangement — Five Different Operations at Five Different Levels." *American Archivist* 27 (January 1964): 21–41.

Johnson, L. Rebecca. *A Guide to the Papers of Senator John J. Williams of Delaware*. Newark: University of Delaware Library, 1990.

Kepley, David R. "Sampling in Archives: A Review." *American Archivist* 47 (Summer 1984): 237–242.

Kimmitt, J. Stanley, and Richard A. Baker. *Conference on the Research Use and Disposition of Senators' Papers Proceedings*. Washington, D.C.: United States Senate, 1978.

Leahy, Emmett J. "Reduction of Public Records." *American Archivist* 3 (January 1940): 13–38.

Lewinson, Paul. "Archival Sampling," *American Archivist* 20 (October 1957): 308–309.

Library of Congress. *Library of Congress Subject Headings*. Washington, D.C.: Library of Congress, 1990.

_____. Central Services Division. *A Guide for the Creation, Organization and Maintenance of Records in Congressional Offices.* Washington, D.C.: Library of Congress, revised 1991.

Linke, Daniel J. *Oral History Project: Procedure Manual.* Norman, OK: Carl Albert Congressional Research and Studies Center, 1990.

Lovett, Robert W. "The Appraisal of Older Business Records." *American Archivist* 15 (April 1952): 231–239.

Lucas, Lydia. "Managing Congressional Papers: A Repository View." *American Archivist* 41 (July 1978): 275–280.

Lyndon Baines Johnson Library. *Historical Materials in the Lyndon Baines Johnson Library.* Austin, TX: Lyndon Baines Johnson Library, 1988.

Mackaman, Frank H. *Congressional Papers Project Report.* Washington, D.C.: National Historical Publications and Records Commission, 1986.

_____. "Managing Case Files in Congressional Collections: The Hazard of Prophecy." *The Midwestern Archivist* 4 (1979): 95–104.

McKay, Eleanor. "Random Sampling Techniques: A Method of Reducing Large, Homogeneous Series in Congressional Papers." *American Archivist* 41 (July 1978): 281–289.

Mathews, Janice, and Todd Kosmerick. "SAA Congressional Papers Roundtable Presentation on Collection Development Policy and Deed of Gift." Society of American Archivist Annual Meeting, September 1993, unpublished.

Melvin, L. Rebecca Johnson. "Congressional Papers Conference, Portland, Maine, 1994." Society of American Archivists Congressional Papers Roundtable *Newsletter* (November 1994): 2–3.

Miller, Cynthia Pease, editor-in-chief. *A Guide to Research Collections of Former Members of the United States House of Representatives, 1789–1987.* House Doc. 100-171. Washington, D.C.: United States House of Representatives, 1988.

_____. "Guidelines for the Dispositon of Members' Papers." United States House of Representatives Historical Office, 1991.

Miller, Frederic M. *Arranging and Describing Archives and Manuscripts.* Chicago: Society of American Archivists, 1990.

Minnesota Historical Society, Division of Library and Archives. "Report of the Congressional Papers Appraisal Committee." 1993.

Moore, Michael T. *The Jack Hightower Papers.* Waco, TX: Baylor University Political Collections, 1989, rev. 1990.

National Archives and Records Administration. "Managing Electronic Records Instructional Guide." Washington, D.C.: NARA, 1990.

_____. "Standards for Management of Federal Records Created or Received on Electronic Mail Systems." *Code of Federal Regulations* 36, Part 1234, 1994.

_____. "Strategic Plan for Information Systems and Technology, Fiscal Years 1991–1995." Washington, DC: NARA, 1990.

_____, Advisory Committee on the Records of Congress. *Report.* Washington, D.C.: NARA, 1991; *second report*, 1995.

Nelson, Naomi L., creator. "Sam Nunn Congressional Collection Database Description." Special Collections, Robert W. Woodruff Library. Atlanta, GA: Emory University, revised October 1993.

Paul, Karen Dawley. *The Documentation of Congress: Report of the Congressional Archivists Roundtable Task Force on Congressional Documentation*. S. Pub. 102-20. Washington, D.C.: United States Senate, 1992.

_____, compiler. *Guide to Research Collections of Former United States Senators, 1789–1995*. S. Pub. 103–35. Washington, D.C.: United States Senate, 1995.

_____. *Records Managment Handbook for United States Senate Committees*. S. Pub. 100-5. Washington, D.C.: United States Senate, 1988.

_____. *Records Management Handbook for United States Senators and Their Repositories*. 2nd edition. Washington, D.C.: United States Senate, 1992.

Peterson, Gary M., and Trudy Huskamp Peterson. *Archives and Manuscripts Law*. Chicago: Society of American Archivists, 1985.

Peterson, Trudy H. "The Deed and The Gift." *American Archivist* 42 (January 1979): 61–66.

Phillips, Faye. "Congressional Papers Collection Development Policies." *American Archivist* 58 (Summer 1995).

_____. "Developing Collecting Policies for Manuscript Collections." *American Archivist* 47 (Winter 1984): 30–42.

_____. "Harper's Ferry Revisited: The Role of Congressional Staff Archivists in Implementing the Congressional Papers Project Report." *Provenance* 6 (Spring 1988): 26–44.

_____. *Local History Collections in Libraries*. Englewood, CO: Libraries Unlimited, 1995.

_____ and Merna W. Ford. *Russell B. Long Collection Guide*. Baton Rouge, LA: Louisiana State University Libraries, 1995.

Pugh, Mary Jo. *Providing Reference Services for Archives and Manuscripts*. Chicago: Society of American Archivists, 1992.

Rare Books and Manuscripts Section, American Library Association. *Genre Terms: A Thesaurus for Use in Rare Book and Special Collections Cataloging*. Chicago: American Library Association, 1990.

_____. *Provenance Evidence: Thesaurus for Use in Rare Book and Special Collections Cataloging*. Chicago: American Library Association, 1990.

_____. *Relator Terms for Rare Book, Manuscript and Special Collections Cataloging*. Chicago: American Library Association, 1990. See also the *Form Terms for Archives and Manuscript Control*, from the Research Libraries Group.

Ritzenthaler, Mary Lynn. *Preserving Archives and Manuscripts*. Chicago: Society of American Archivists, 1993.

_____, Gerald J. Munoff, and Margery S. Long. *Archives & Manuscripts: Administration of Photographic Collections*. Chicago: Society of American Archivists, 1984.

Rogers, Ben. "Baylor Collections of Political Materials Collection Development Policy." Waco, TX: Baylor University, May 1994.

Schellenberg, Theodore R. *Modern Archives: Principles and Techniques*. Chicago: University of Chicago Press, 1958.

Sly, Margery N. "Access to Congressional Case Files: Survey of Practices, Implications for Use." Unpublished paper, ca. 1987.

Tabbert, Barbara M. *Guide to the Mike Gravel Papers, 1957–1980*. Fairbanks, AK: University of Alaska–Fairbanks, Elmer E. Rasmuson Library, 1986.

Trost, Maxine. *Archives and Manuscripts OCLC Cataloging Manual.* Laramie, WY: American Heritage Center, 1991.

_____. *Archives and Manuscripts Processing Manual.* Laramie, WY: American Heritage Center, 1991.

United States House of Representatives, Committee on House Administration. *Guidelines for Standing and Select Committees in the Preparation, Filing, Archiving and Disposal of Committee Records.* Washington, D.C.: Government Printing Office, 1990.

Vogt, Sheryl. "Processing Manual, Richard B. Russell Library for Political Research and Studies." Athens, GA: University of Georgia Libraries, 1994.

Index